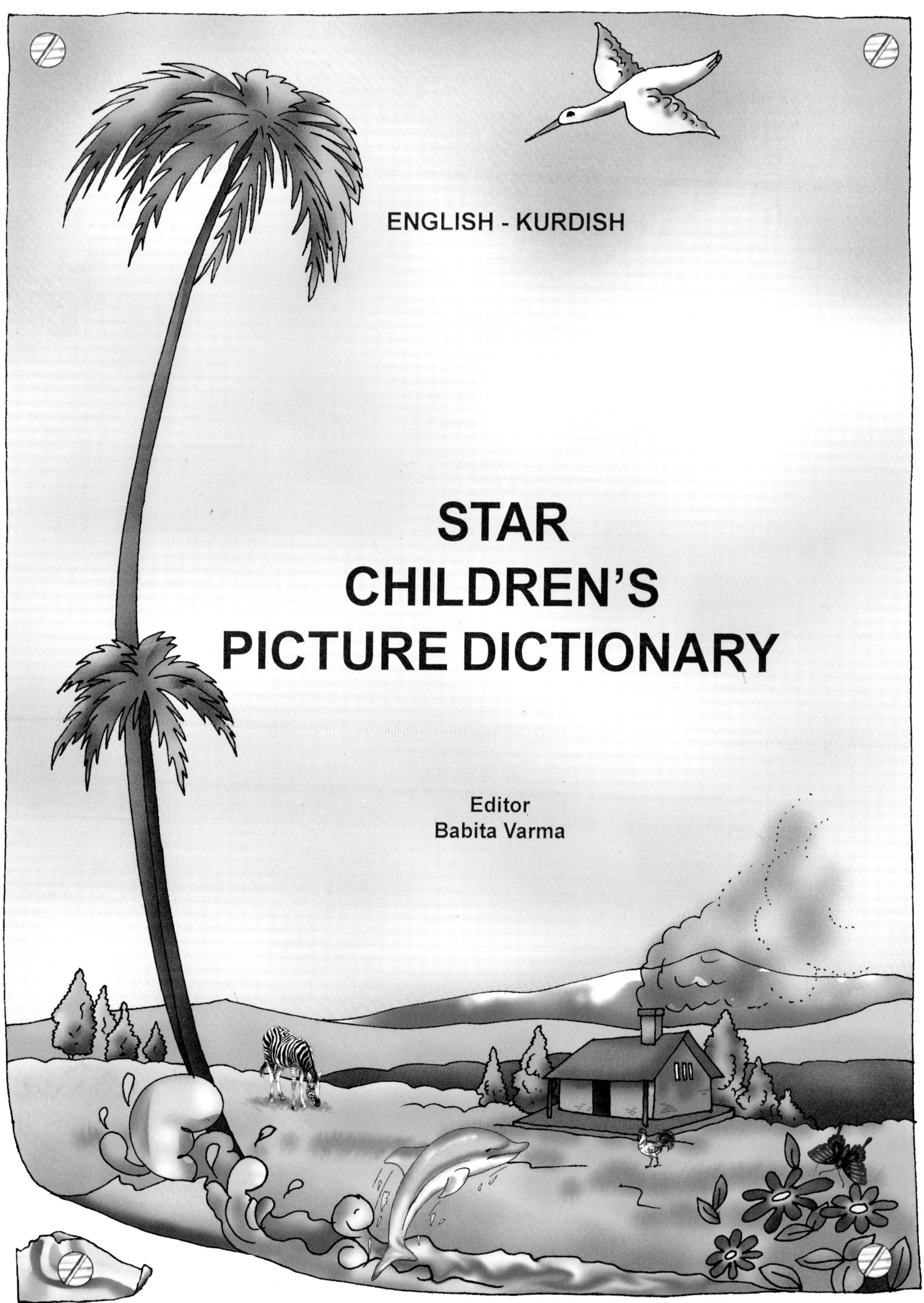

ENGLISH - KURDISH

STAR CHILDREN'S PICTURE DICTIONARY

Editor
Babita Varma

STAR CHILDREN'S PICTURE DICTIONARY

Varma, Babita (Editor)

Published by :

STAR PUBLICATIONS PVT. LTD.
Asaf Ali Road, New Delhi-110002 (INDIA)
email : starpub@satyam.net.in

Revised Edition : 2005

ISBN : 81-7650-071-2

THIS DICTIONARY
has been published in Arabic, Bengali, Chinese, Croation, Danish, Farsi, Gujarati, Hindi, Vietnamese, Malayalam, Norwegian, Punjabi, Portuguese, Somali, Spanish, Tamil, Turkish and Urdu. Other languages are in press.

To
Children of all ages;
whatever language
they speak.

FROM THE PUBLISHERS :

This unique colourful dictionary was first published in 1993, and was brought out in sololingual, bilingual and trilingual editions. Within a span of three years we could publish it in about 32 major languages of the world, and the Dictionary was acclaimed as one of the best pictorial dictionaries to teach various languages-not only to young children but also to those foreigners who wish to learn another language. It was acknowledged as a source to build wordpower and stimulate learning, specially among children.

However, on the basis of various suggestions received since its publication, the Editor decided to revise the whole dictionary by adding many new words and illustrations, as also changing the style. We are now pleased to present this dictionary with a new format. This dictionary now consists of over 1,000 words and colourful illustrations, which have been catagorised in 12 popular subjects. In case of bilingual editions, each word has been translated into the other language, and transliterated where necessary.

We are confident that readers will find this dictionary as a very useful presentation which will encourage browsing, and make learning fun for the young and old alike. Since this dictionary has been published in several languages of the world, it will be found as a timely contribution to multilingualism and multiculturalism.

INDEX

ALPHABET

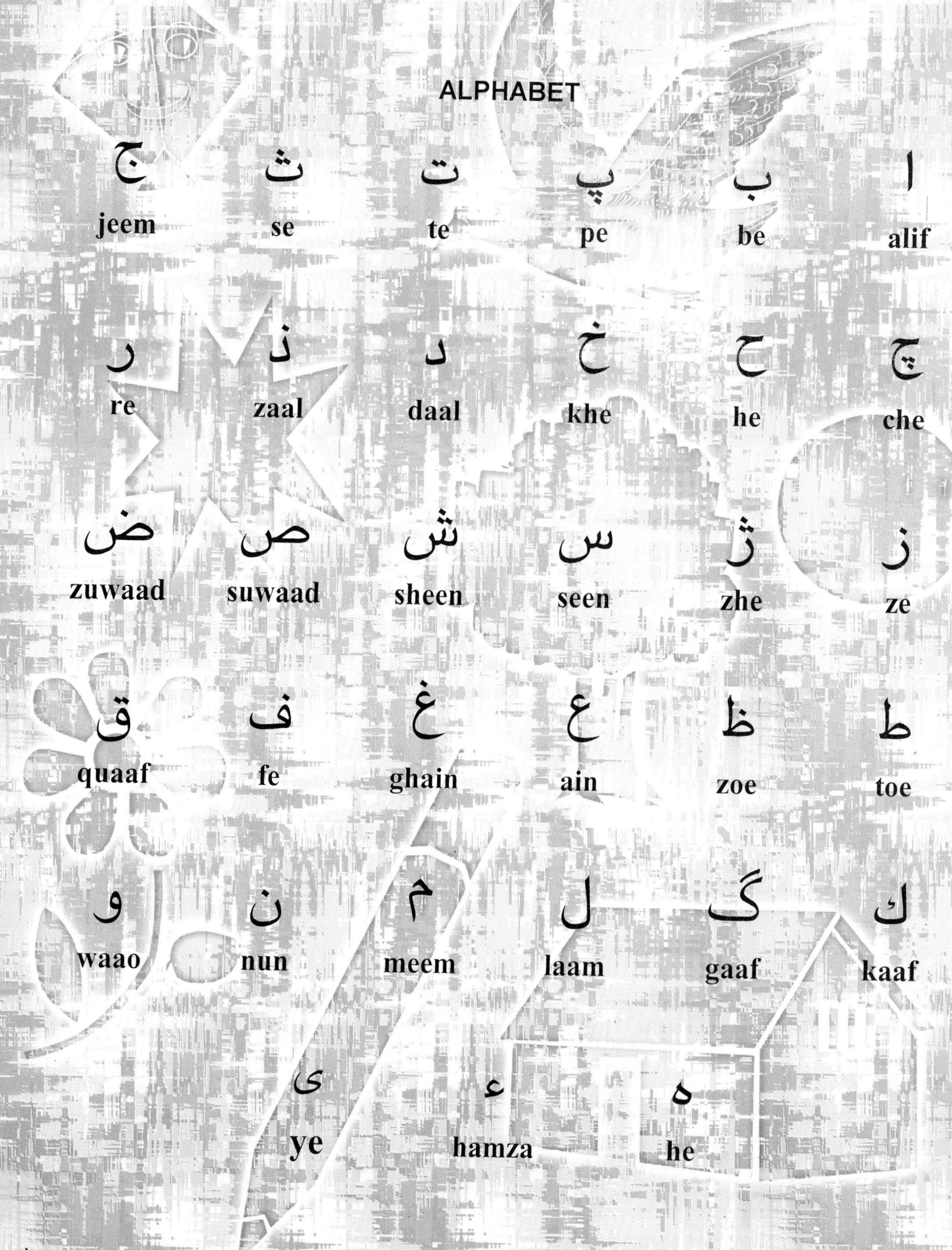

ج	ث	ت	پ	ب	ا
jeem	se	te	pe	be	alif
ر	ذ	د	خ	ح	چ
re	zaal	daal	khe	he	che
ض	ص	ش	س	ژ	ز
zuwaad	suwaad	sheen	seen	zhe	ze
ق	ف	غ	ع	ظ	ط
quaaf	fe	ghain	ain	zoe	toe
و	ن	م	ل	گ	ك
waao	nun	meem	laam	gaaf	kaaf
	ی	ء	ه		
	ye	hamza	he		

A a B b C c D d
E e F f G g H h
I i J j K k L l
M m N n O o P p
Q q R r S s T t
U u V v W w X x
Y y Z z

NUMBERS

0 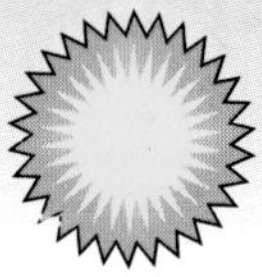 zero - سفر - *sifr*

1  one - یه ك - *yak*

2  two - دوو - *doo*

3  three - سێ - *se*

4  four - چووار - *chowar*

5  five - پێنج - *penj*

6 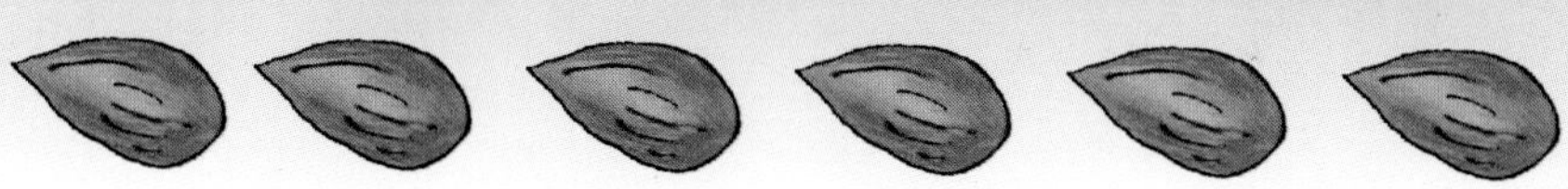 six - شه ش - *shash*

7  seven - حه و ت - *hawt*

8  eight - هه شت - *hasht*

9  nine - نۆ - *noo*

10  ten - ده - *dah*

ANIMALS, BIRDS AND OTHER LIVING CREATURES

اژالٛ ، بالدٛار و جان له برکانی تر

Ajal, Baldar o Janla Barkani Tar

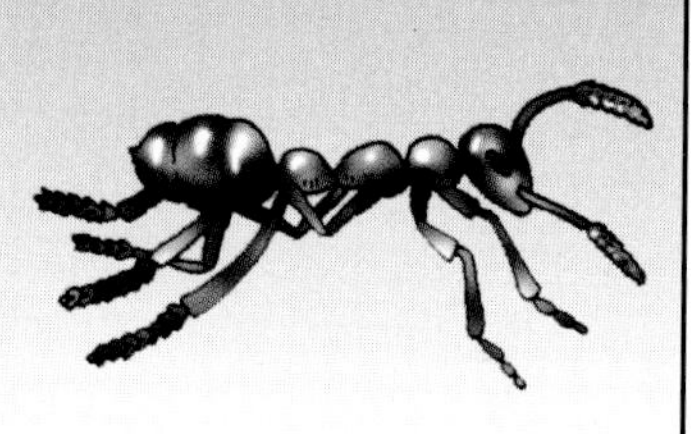

ant

مێرووله

meroula

ape

مه یموون

maimoun

bat

چه ك چه كيله

chak chakila

bear

ورچ

worch

beetle

قالۆچه

ghalocha

bee

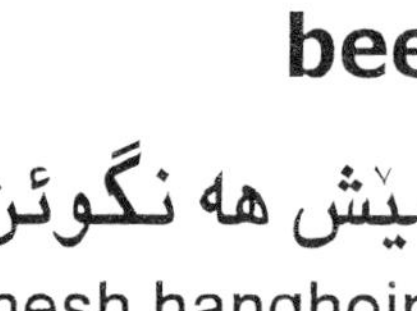

مێش هه نگوئن

mesh hanghoin

bird

بالٚنده

balanda

bison

بووفالۆ

bofalo

buffalo

گای کوهان دار

ghay kohandar

bull

گای نێر

ghay ner

bustard

جوريك باصدار
jorik basder

butterfly
په پۆله
papoula

calf
گوێ لك
goilek

camel
وشتر
woshter

cat
پشیله
peshila

caterpillar
هزار پێ
hezarpei

centipede
هزار پێ
hezarpei

cheetah
ئوزپلێنگ
yozpeling

chickens
جووجكه
jojka

chimpanzee
شامپانزێ
shampanzi

cobra

ماری كۆبرا

mari kobra

cock

كه لە شێر

kalasher

cockroach

قالۆچه

ghalocha

cow

گا-مانگا

ga-manga

crab

دووپشك

dupeshk

crocodile

تيمساح

timsah

crow

قه له ذه ش

ghala rash

cuckoo

فاخته

fakhta

deer

ئاسك

asek

dinosaur

ده ينه سور

daynasor

dog
سه گ
sag

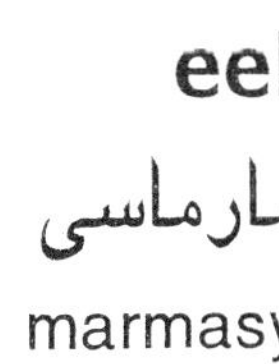

dolphin
دۆلفین
dolphin

donkey
گوێ دریژ
goiderijh

duck
مراوی
moravy

eagle
هه لۆ
halou

eel
مارماسی
marmasy

earthworm
کرمی خاکی
kermikhaki

elephant
فیل
fil

fish
ماسی
masy

flamingos
فلامینگۆ
flamingo

fly

مێش

mesh

fox

ريۆى

riwi

frog

بۆق

bough

giraffe

زه ررافه

zarrafa

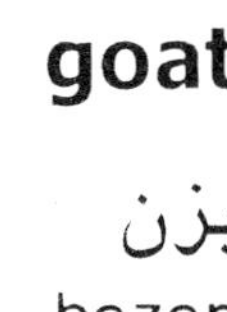

goat

بزن

bezen

goose

قاز

gaz

grasshopper

كولله

kolela

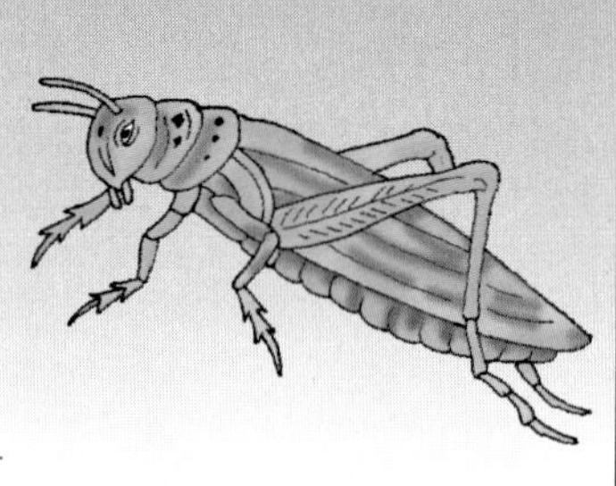

hare

كه روێشك

karoishk

hen

مريشك–مامر

merishk-mamer

heron
ماسی خوار
masikhar

hippopotamus
ئسپی ئاوی
aspi awi

honey-bee
مێش هه نگوئن
mesh hangoun

horse
ئه سپ
asp

insects
مێشووله كان
mesholakan

jackal
چه قه ڵ
chaghal

kangaroo
كانگۆرو
kangaroo

kiwi
باڵنده ی نوك درێژ
balande
nokderijh

ladybird
خاڵ خاڵوكه
khalkhaloka

leopard
پڵنگ
palang

lion

شێر

sher

lizard

مار مێلکه

marmelka

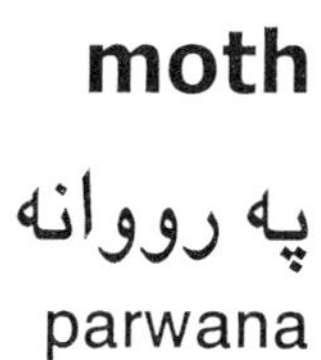

lobster

قرژاڵ

gharjhal

louse

ئسپی

aspe

magpie

قه ڵه رش

ghala rash

monkey

مه یموون

maimoun

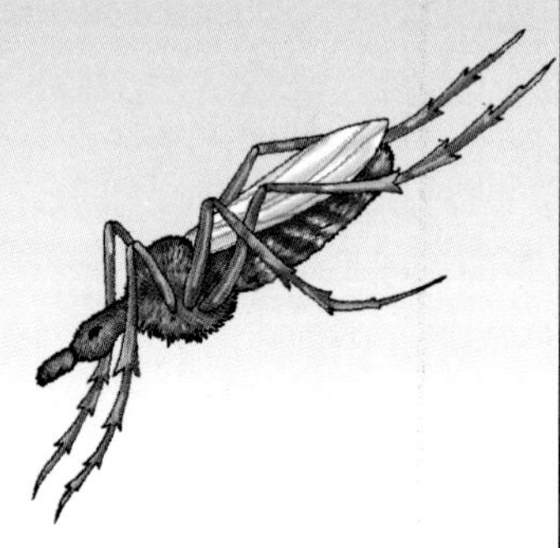

mosquito

مێشووله

meshola

moth

په رووانه

parwana

mouse

مشك

meshk

mule

که ر

kar

myna
مینا
mina

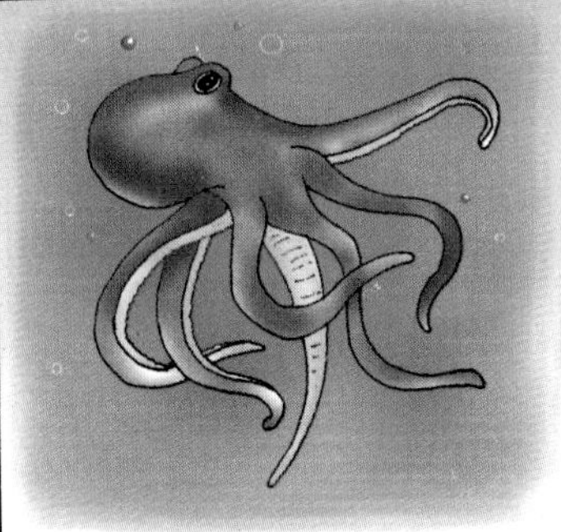

octopus
هه شت پیٚ
hasht pei

ostrich
ووشتر میٚ
woshter me

otter
سموٚر
samour

owl
کوند
kond

ox
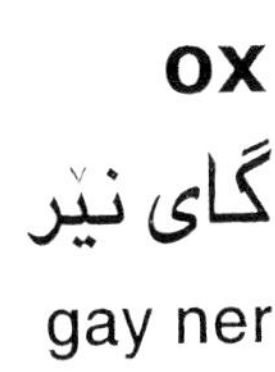
گای نیٚر
gay ner

platypus
پلاتی پوٚس
platipos

panda
ورچی پاندا
worchi panda

panther
یوز پلنگ
yoz palang

parrot
توتی
toti

peacock

تاووس

tavows

pelican

پلی کان

plikan

penguin

به تریق

batrigh

puppy

تۆتکه سه گ

totka sag

pigeon

کۆتر

kowter

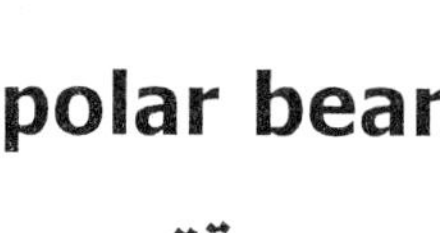

polar bear

ورچی قتبی

worchi ghotbi

porcupine

ژوژك

jho jhak

prawn

مه یگوو

maigo

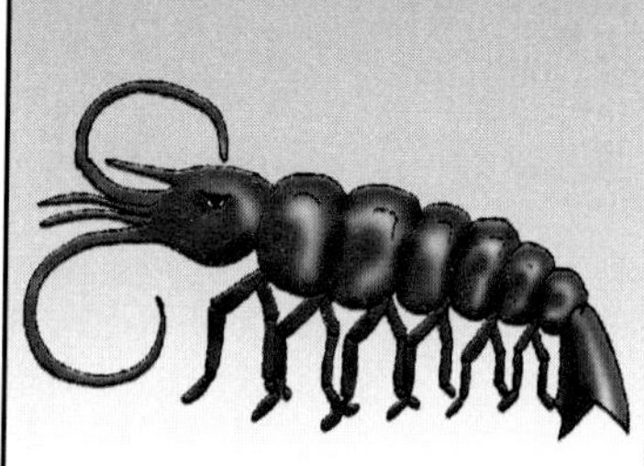

quail

بلدرچین

belderchin

rabbit

که رویشك

karoishk

rat
مشك
meshk

rhinoceros
که رگه ده ن
kargadan

scorpion
دوو پشك
dowpeshk

seal
فۆك
fok

shark
کۆسه
kosa

sheep
مه ڕ
mar

snake
مار
mar

sparrow
چۆله که
cholaka

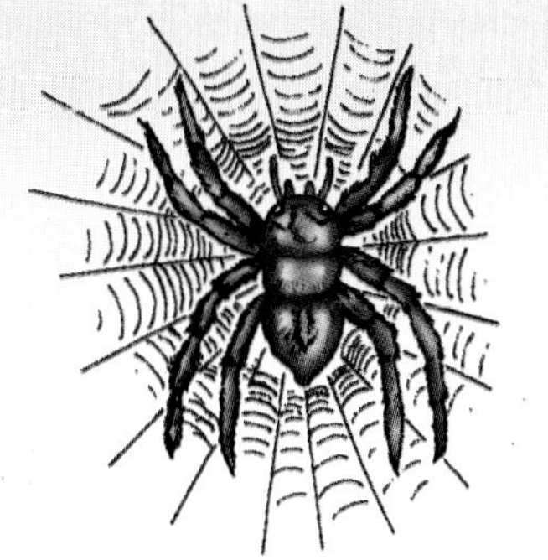

spider
جاڵ جاڵۆکه
jal jaloka

squirrel
سه نجاق
sanjagh

stork

لە ك لە ك

laklak

swan

قوو

ghow

tiger

بە بر

babr

tortoise

كيسە ڵ

kesal

turtle

كيسە ڵ

kesal

vulture

داڵە كە رخۆرە

dalkarkhora

woodpecker

داركوت

darkoot

wolf

گورگ

gorg

yak

گامێش

gamesh

zebra

گۆڕە كە ر

gora kar

FOOD, DRINKS AND OTHER THINGS TO EAT

چێشت ، خواردنه وه ، خواردنه مه نی

Chesht, Khardanawa, Khardanamani

almonds
بادام
badam

apple
سێو
sev

apricot
قه یسی
ghaisy

bananas
مۆز
mouz

beetroot
چه وه نده ر
chavandar

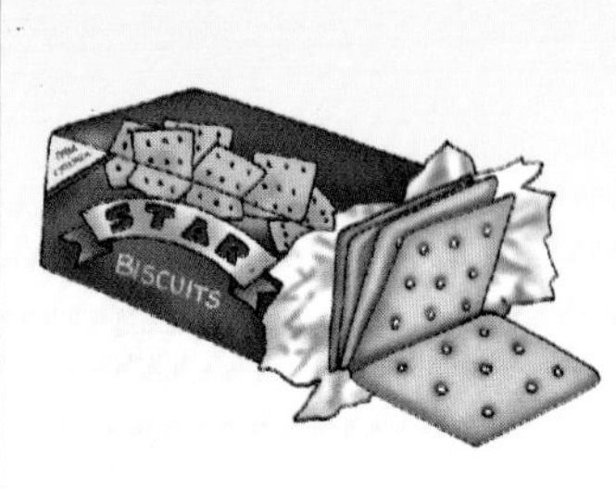

biscuits

بیسکویت
biscuit

bread
نان
nan

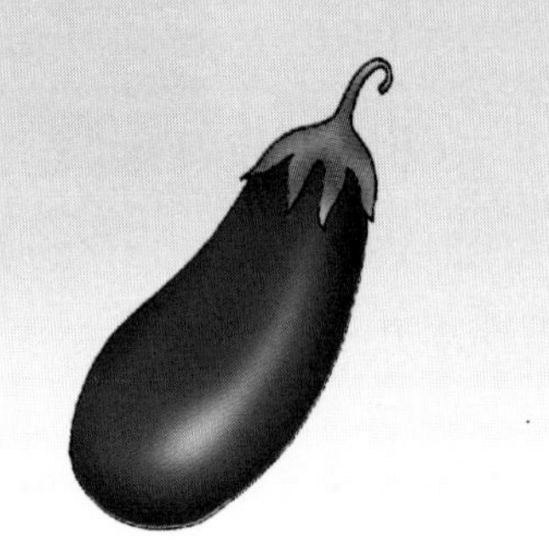

brinjal
باینجان
bayenjan

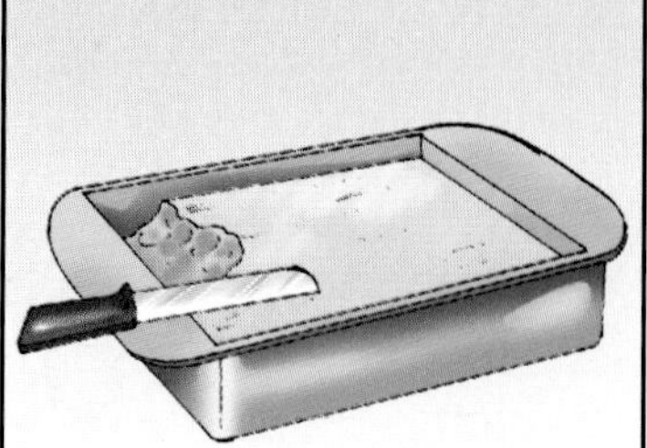

butter
که ره
kara

cabbage
که له م
kalam

cake

کێك

keik

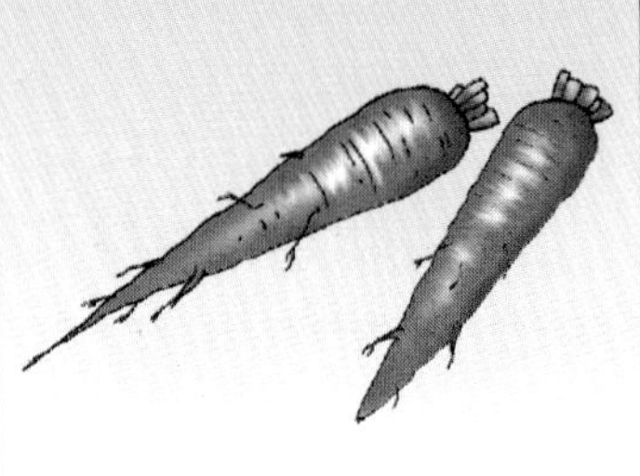

carrots

گێزه ر

geizar

cauliflower

گل که له م

gole kalam

cereal

دانه وێله

danavela

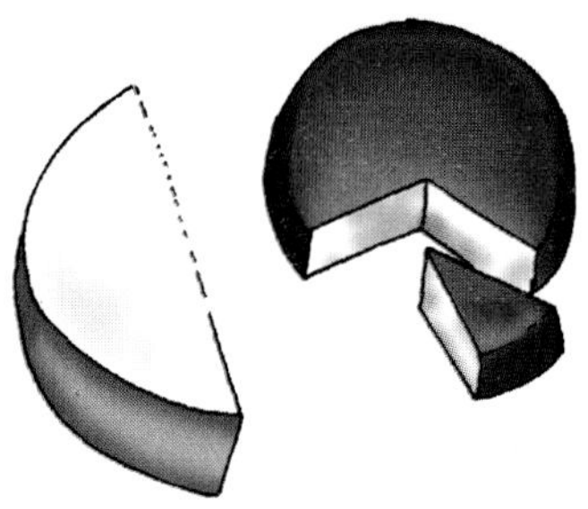

cheese

په نیر

panir

cherries

گیلاس

gelas

chilli

بی باری سوور

bibarisour

chocolate

شۆکۆلات

shokolat

coconut

نارگیل

nargil

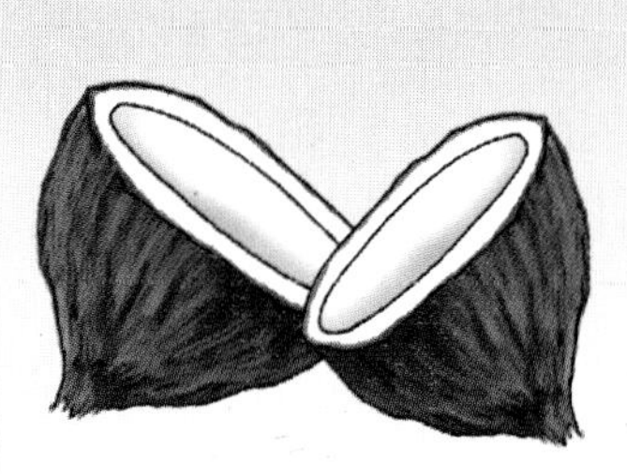

coffee

قاوه

ghava

cucumber
هارۆ
harrow

currants
مێوژ
miojh

dates
خورما
khorma

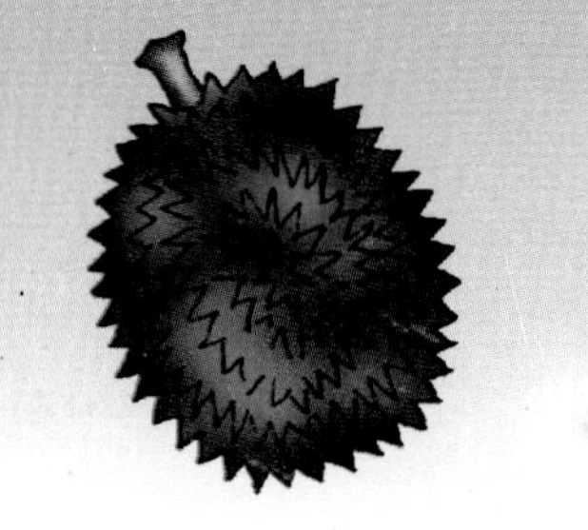

durian
داری قه هوه
darighahva

egg
هێلکه
helka

fig

هه نجیر
hanjir

fruit

میوه
miva

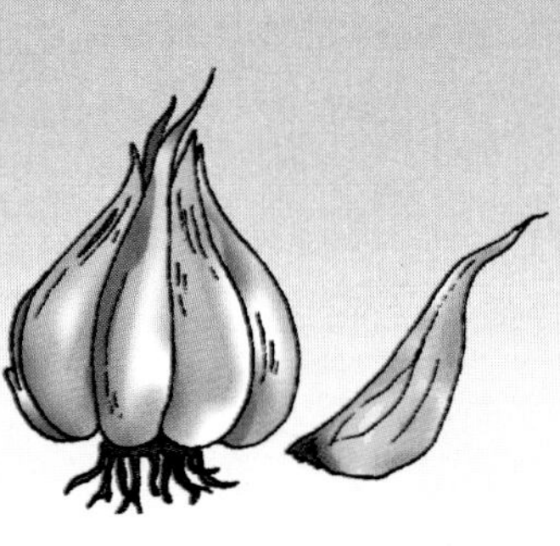

garlic

سیر
sir

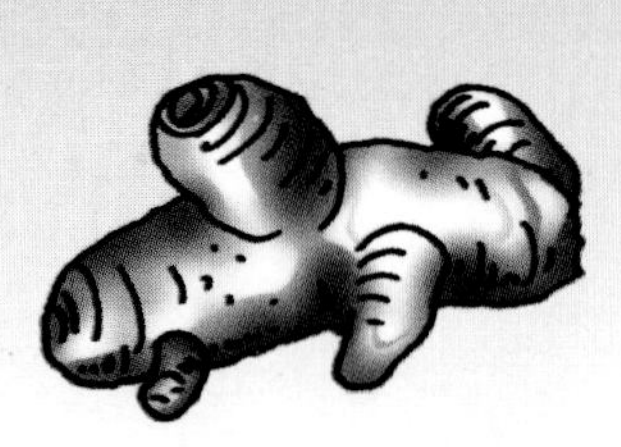

ginger
سێوی بن ئه رزی
sevibenarzi

grapes

ترێ
terii

grapefruit

گری فروت

greyfrot

guava

هه رمێ

harmei

honey

هه نگوین

hangoin

ice-cream

به ستنی

bastani

jackfruit

جۆره دارێك

jora darik

jam

مره با

morabba

jelly

ژێللێ

jilly

ladyfinger

بامێ

bamy

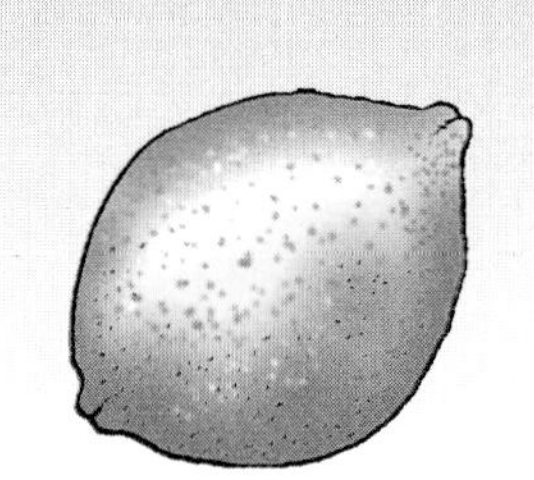

lemon

لیمۆ

limoo

lettuce

كاهو

kahoo

mango
ئه نبه
anba

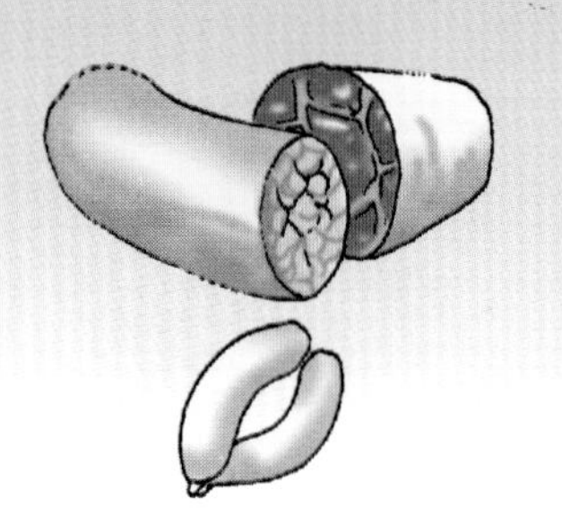

meat
گۆشت
gosht

melon
کاڵه ك
kalak

milk
شیر
shir

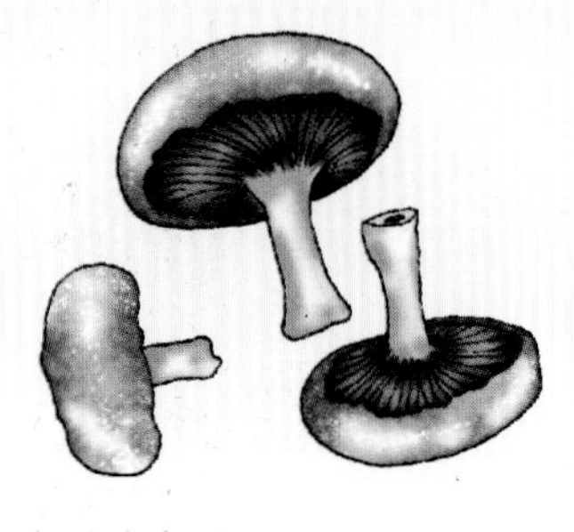

mushrooms
کارگ
karg

mustard
خه رده ڵ
khardal

mutton
گۆشتی مه ڕێ
goshti mare

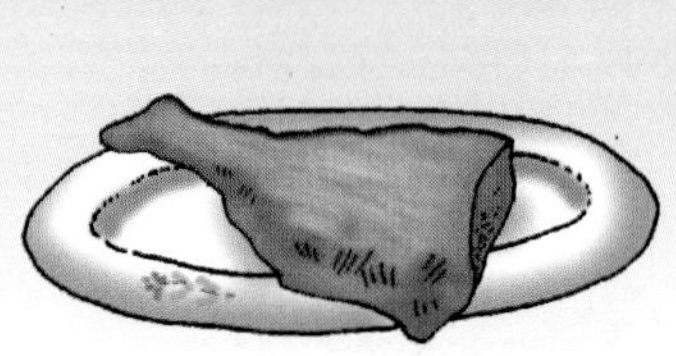

orange
پرته قاڵ
pertaghal

papaya
ئه نبه ی هندی
anbe hendi

passion fruit
جوريك ميوه
jorik miva

peach

خوق

ghoukh

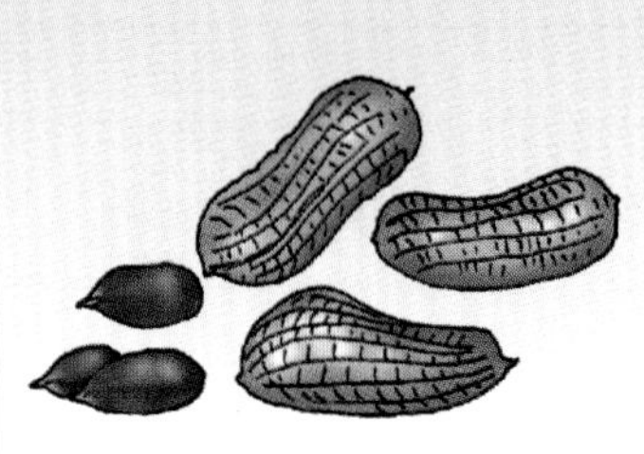

peanuts

پاقله ی سودانی

pagheley soudany

pear

هه رم ی

harmei

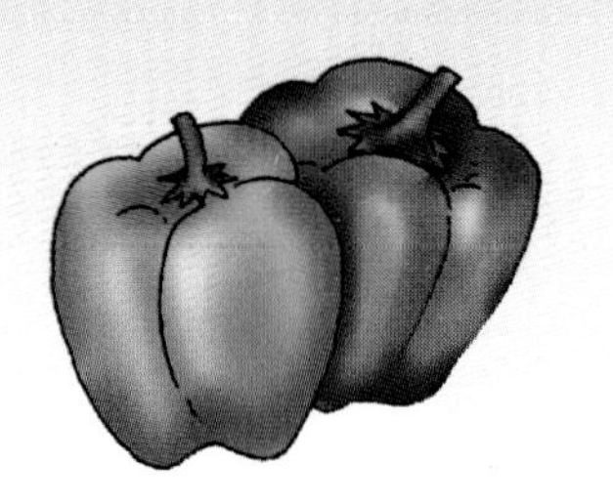

peppers

بی به ر

bibar

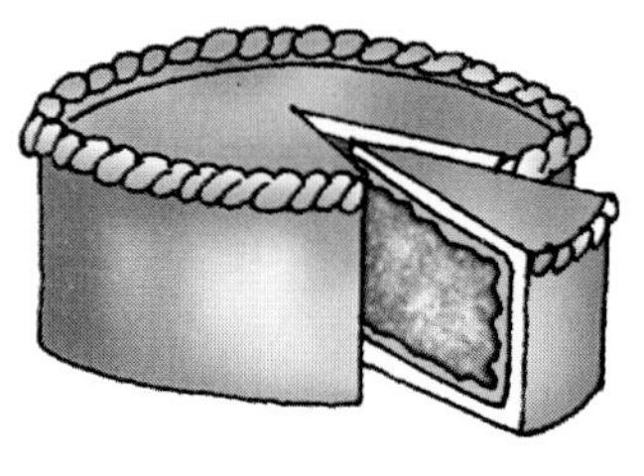

pie

بوره ك

bourak

pineapple

ئاناناس

ananas

potatoes

ئه رئالماسی

yeralmasi

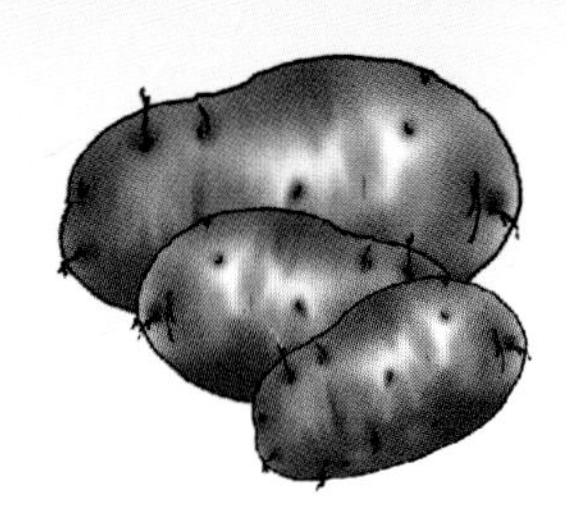

pumpkin

كولّه كه تنبه ل

kolaka tanbal

plums

ئالوبخارا

alow bokhara

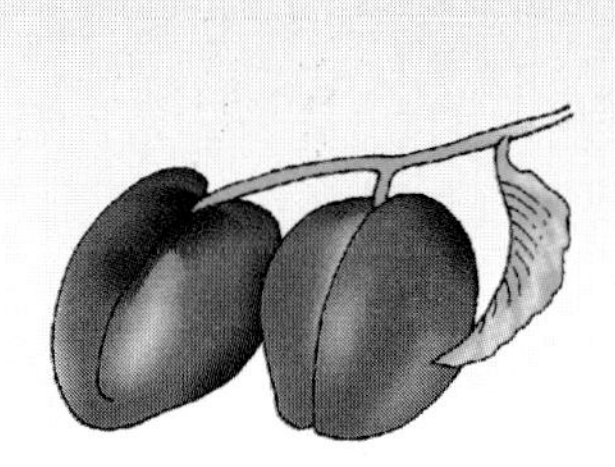

pudding

پودینگ

poding

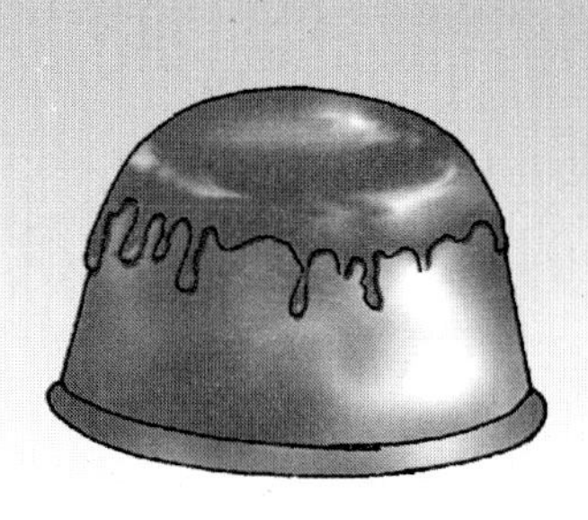

radishes
توری سۆر
torisor

raisins
کشمش
keshmesh

raspberries
ته مشك
tameshk

rice
برنج
berenj

salad
ساڵاد
salad

salt

خوێ
khoy

sandwich
ساندویچ
sandwich

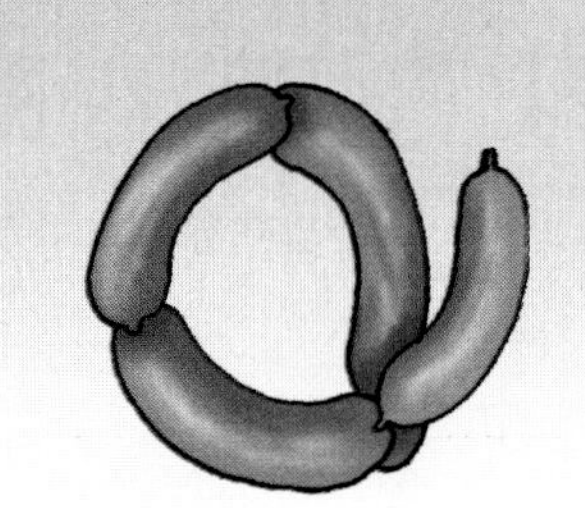

sausages
سۆسیس
sosis

soup
سووپ
sop

soyabeans
دانه ی سۆیا
daneysoya

spaghetti

ماكارۆنى

makarony

spinach

ئپ سپه ناغ

aspanagh

strawberries

شڵيك

shalik

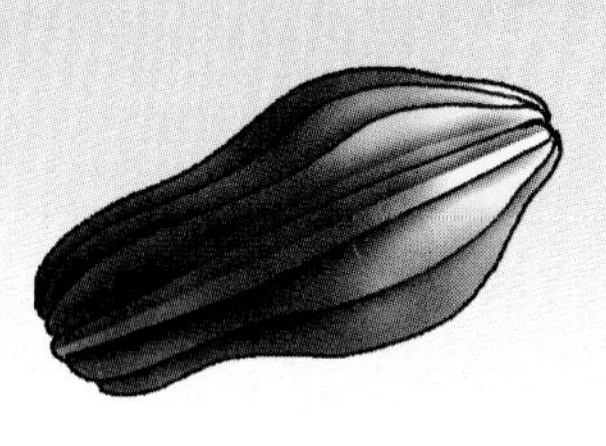

starfruit

جوريك ميوه

jorik miva

sugar

شه كه ر

shakar

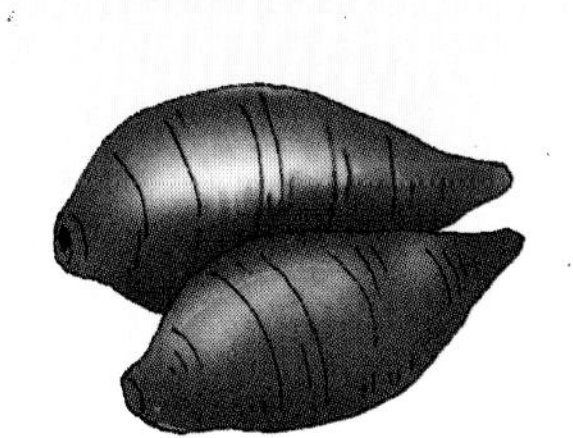

یه ره ڵماسی په شه نگی

yeralmasi pashangy

شيرنى

shirni

sweetcorn

شه ردارى

sarday

syrup

شه ربه ت

sharbat

چاى

chay

toast
نانی تۆست
nani tost

toffees
تافی
taffy

tomato
ته ماته
tamata

turnip
شه لْقه م
shalgham

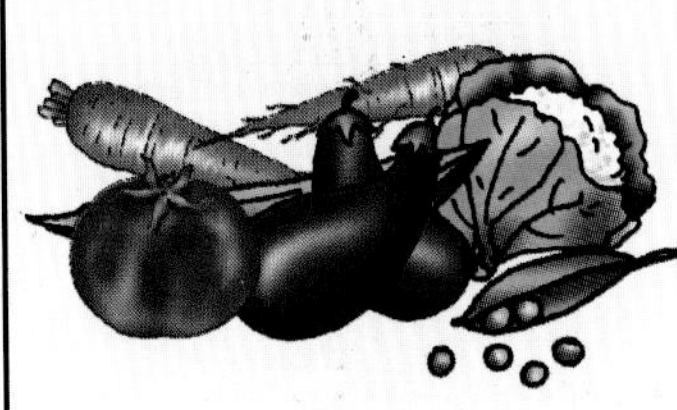

vegetables
سه وزه وات
savzawat

walnut

گوێز
goiz

water
ئاو
av

watermelon
شوتی
showty

wheat
گه نم
ganem

yoghurt
ماست
mast

HOME

مالٚ

Mal

antenna

ئانتێن

antin

balcony

هه یوان

haiwan

basin

دسشۆر

das shour

bathroom

حه مام

hamam

bed

ته ختی نووستین

takhti nousten

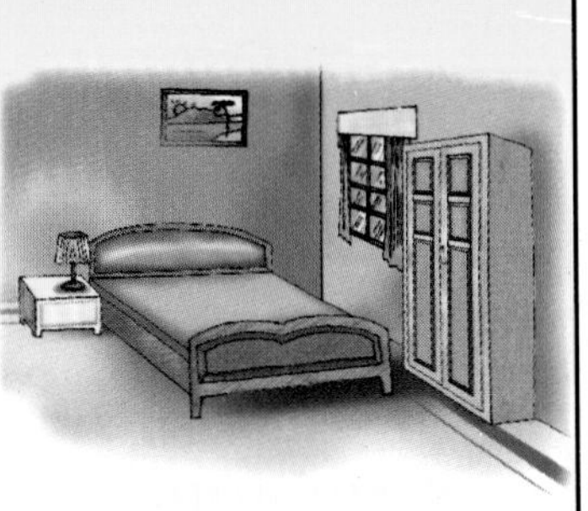

bedroom

ژووری خه وی

jhory khave

bench

کورسی درێژ

korsy derijh

blanket

په تو

pato

bucket

سه تڵ

satl

cabinet

کابێنت

kabinet

carpet
فه رش
farsh

ceiling
میچ
mich

chair
کورسی
koursy

chandelier
چرای لووستر
cheray looster

chimneys
دووکه ڵ کێش
dokalkesh

cloth
پارچه
parcha

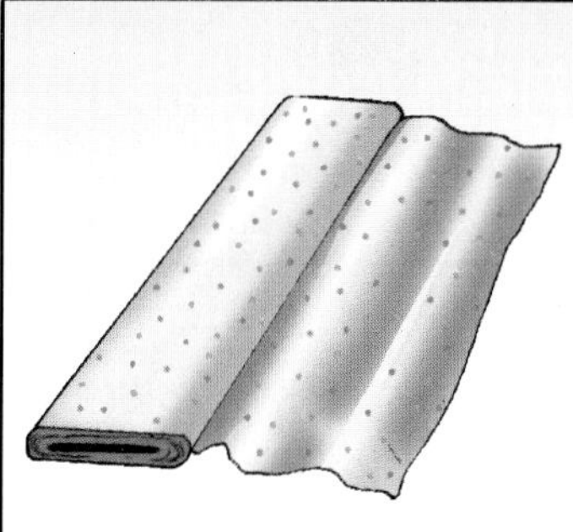

cot
لانکه
lanka

cupboard
دۆلاب
dowlab

curtains
په رده
parda

door
ده رکه
darka

drain

پلوسك

plosk

elevator

بالـّابه ر

balabar

escalator

پلی کانی به رقی

pelikani barghy

fences

په رچین

parchin

flats

ته خت

takht

flower vase

گولدان

goldan

foam

هه ور

hawr

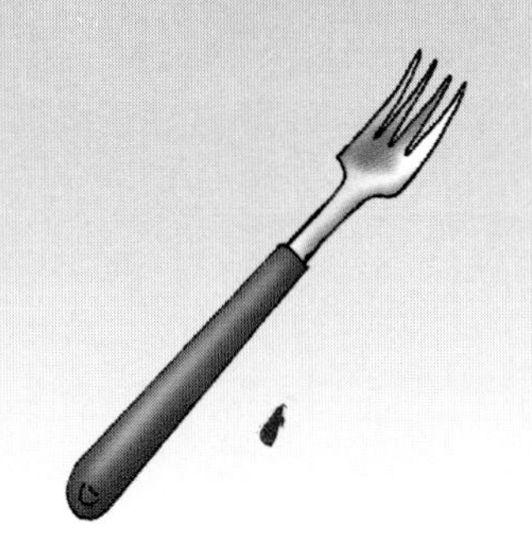

fork

چه نگالّ

changal

garden

باغچه

baghcha

garage

گاراژ

garage

gate
درگا
darga

home
ماڵ
mal

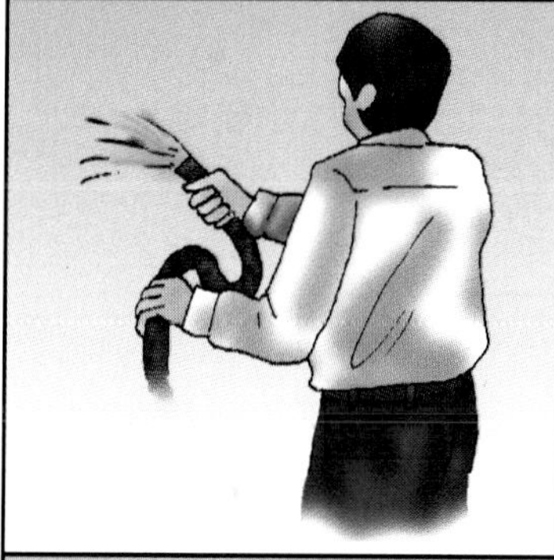

hose
شیلانگی ئاو
shilangi av

kitchen
چێست خانه
chestkhana

letter-box
جه عبی نامه
jabei nama

mattress
دۆشکی خه وێ
doushaky khawe

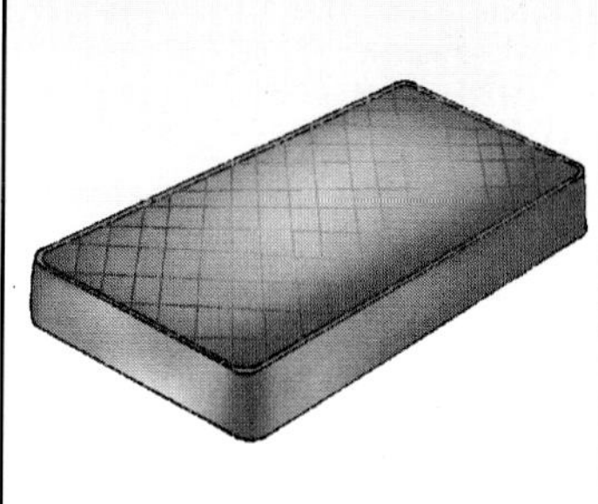

matchbox
شه مچه
shamcha

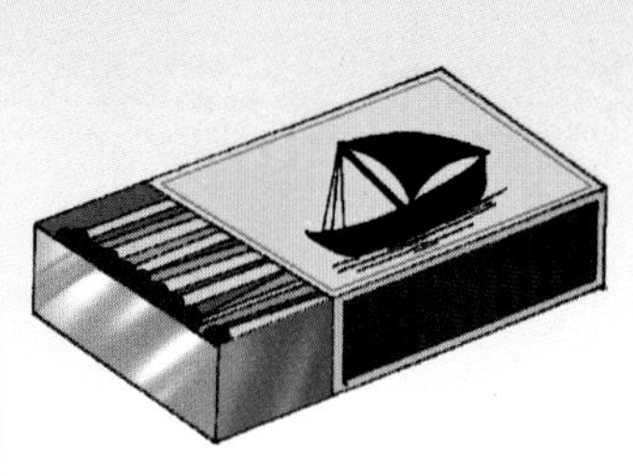

mop
گه سك
gask

necktie
کراوات
kerawat

oven
فێری گازی
feri gazi

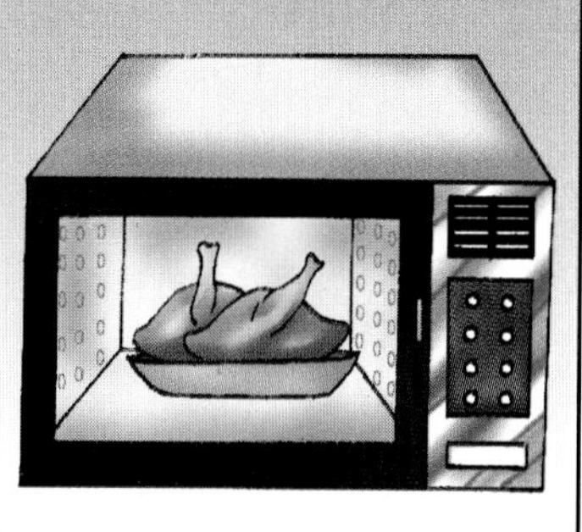

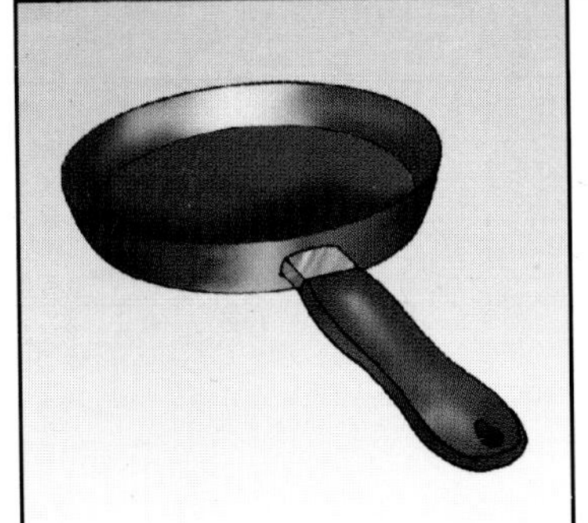

pan

تاوه

tawa

plate

ده وری

dawri

pram

کاسکه ی مندالّ

kaleske mendal

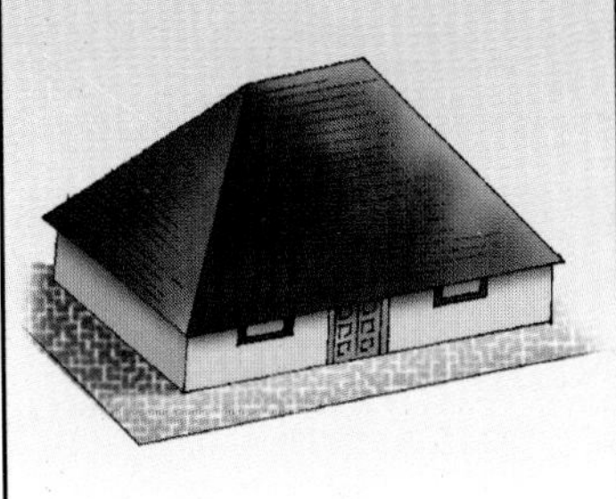

roof

سه ربان

sarban

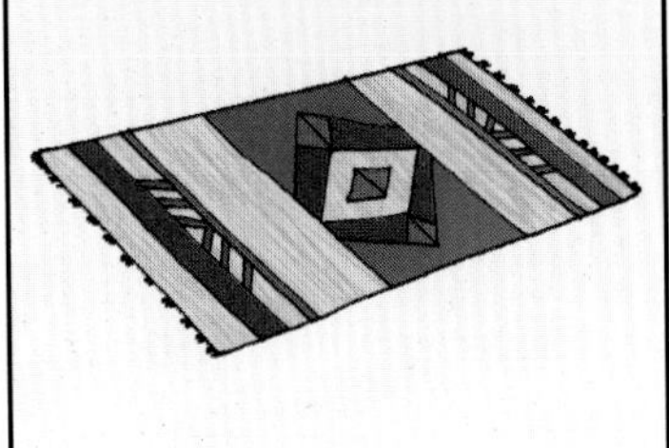

rug

قالیچه

ghalicha

sewing machine

مه کینه

makina

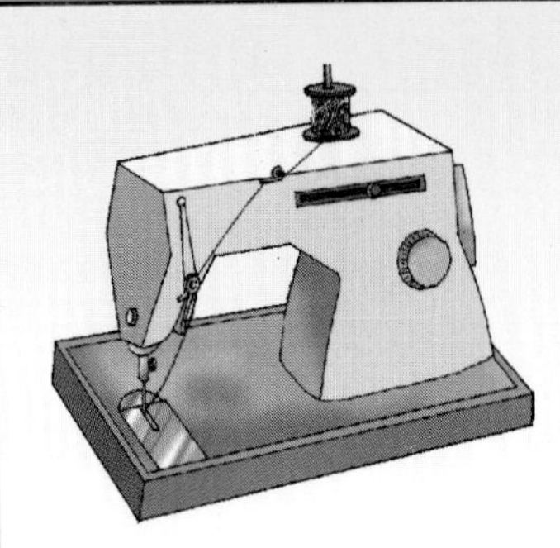

seats

جێگا

jiga

shelf

گه نجه

ganja

shower

دووش

dowsh

sink

قاب شۆر

ghabshour

smoke
دووكه لّ
doukal

sofa
موبلّى راحتى
mobli rahati

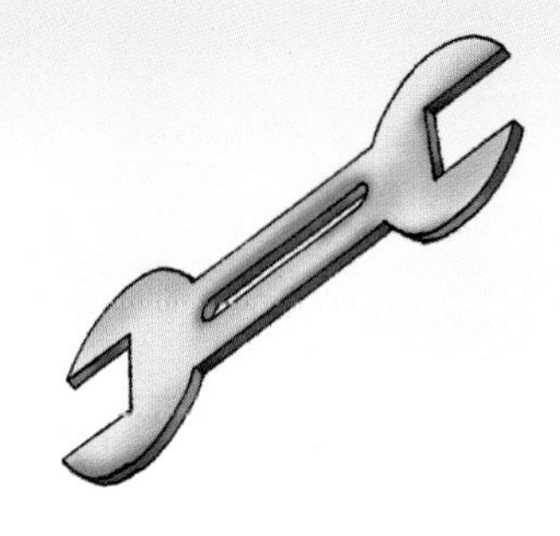

spanner
ئاچه ر
achar

stairs/steps
پليكان
pelican

toilet
ئاو ده ست
av dast

toothbrush
مسواك
meswak

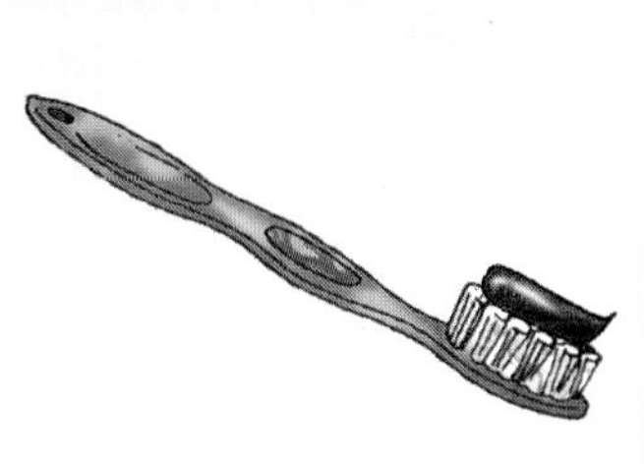

tub
وان
wan

wall
ديوار
dewar

wardrobe
كمد
komod

window
په نجه ره
panjara

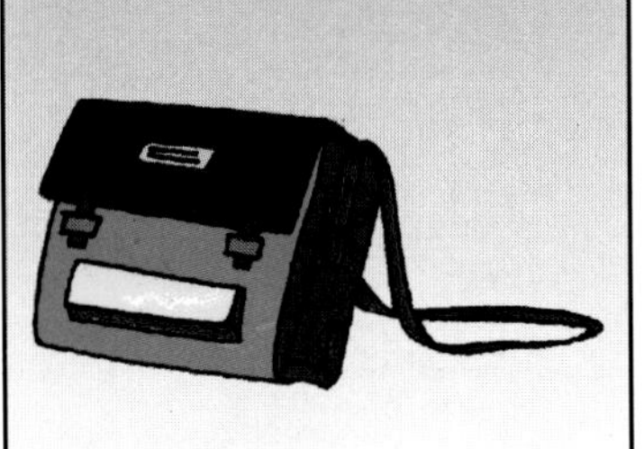

bag
كيف
kif

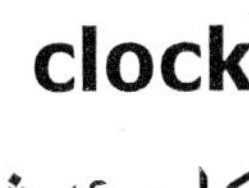

clock
كات ئه ژمێر
kat ajhmir

glass
ليوان
liwan

cushions
بالێنج
balenj

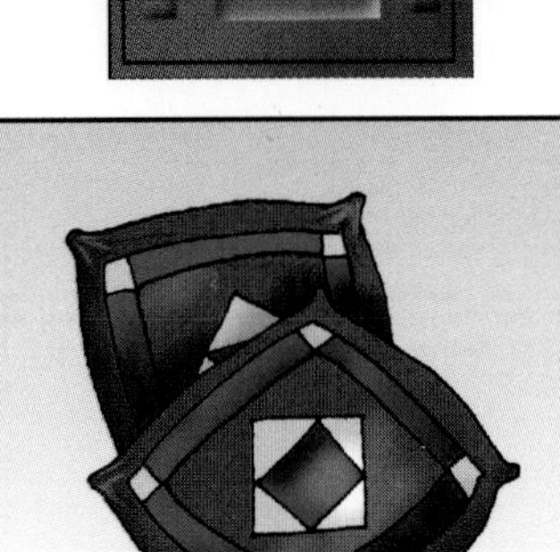

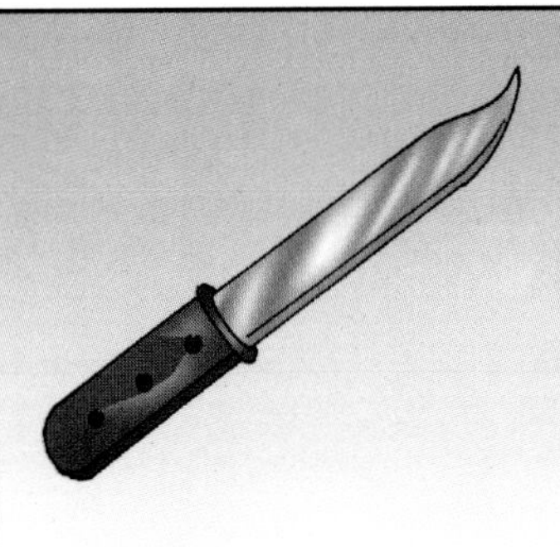

knife
چه قۆ
chaghow

radio
راديو
radiu

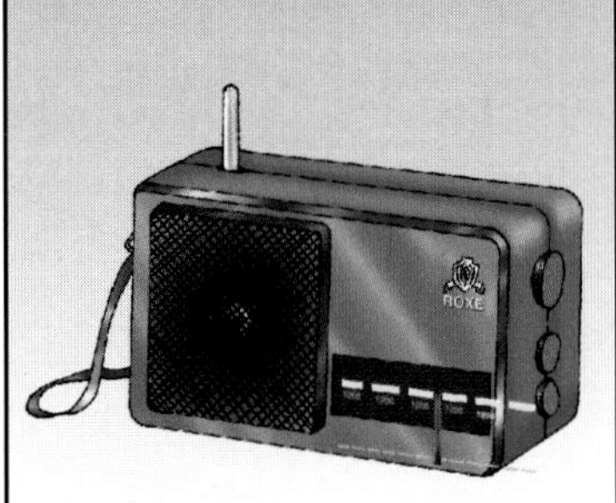

refrigerator
يه خچاڵ
yakhchal

telephone
تيلفۆن
tilfon

stove
چرای چێشت لێنان
cheray chesht lenan

table
مێز
miz

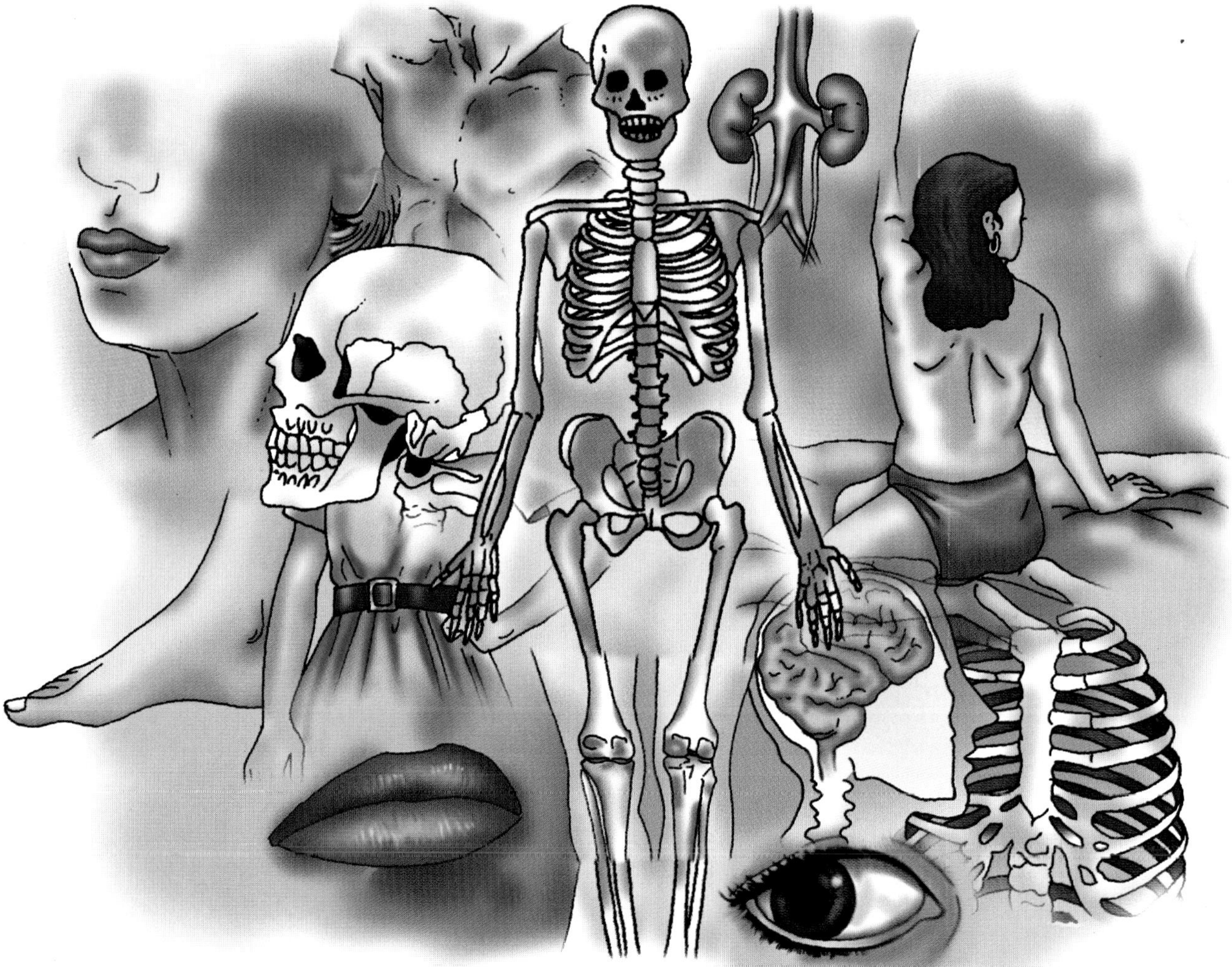

HUMAN BODY

ئاندامی مرۆڤ

Andami Maroof

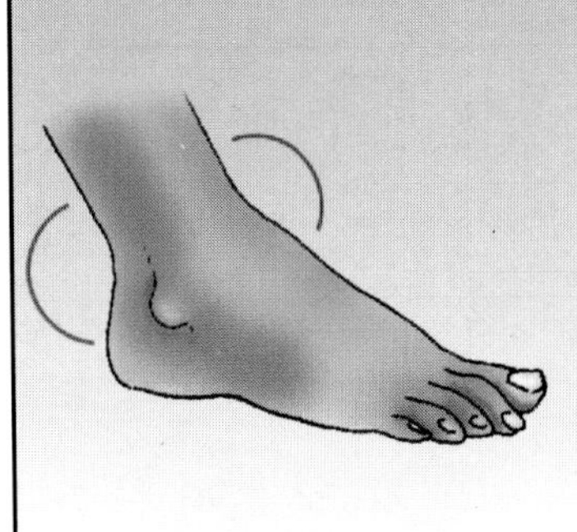

ankle

گوێزینگ

goizing

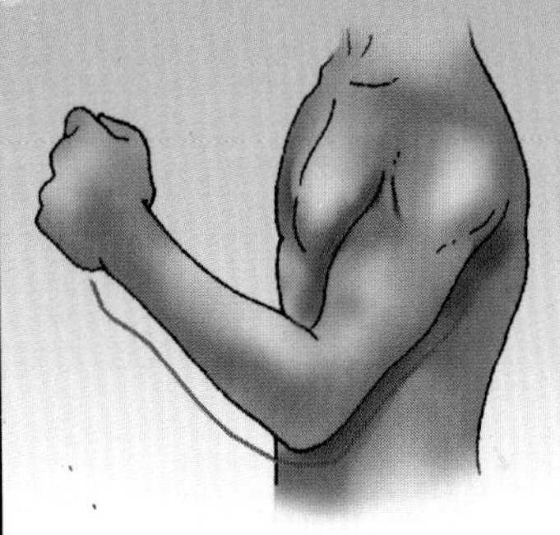

arm

باسك

bask

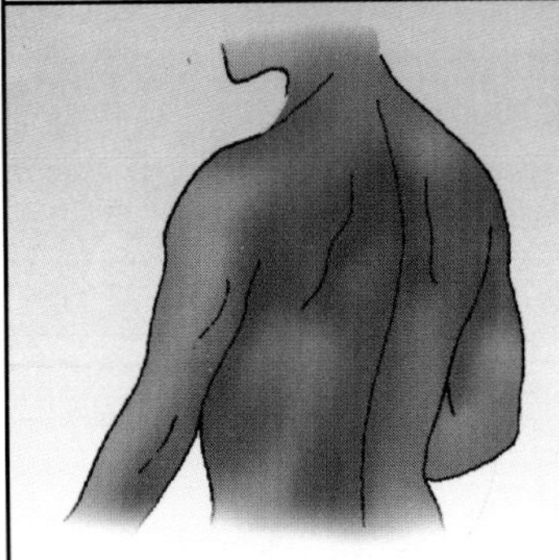

back

پشت

pesht

beard

ردێن

redden

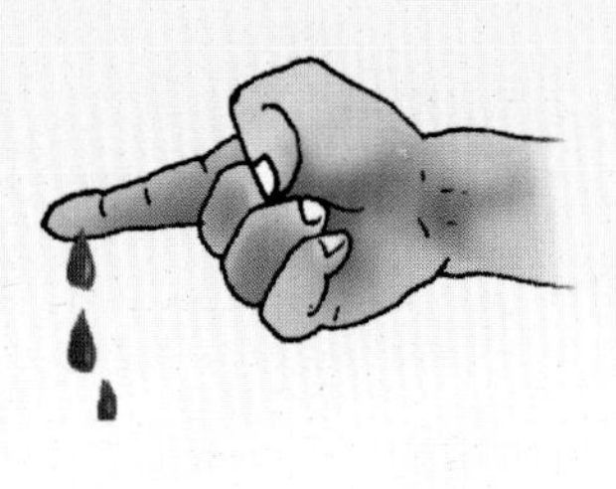

blood

خوێن

khoin

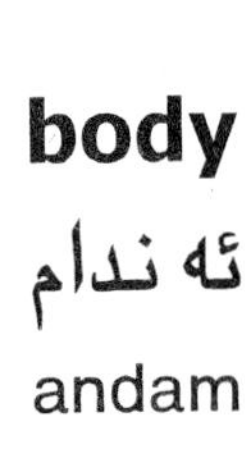

body

ئه ندام

andam

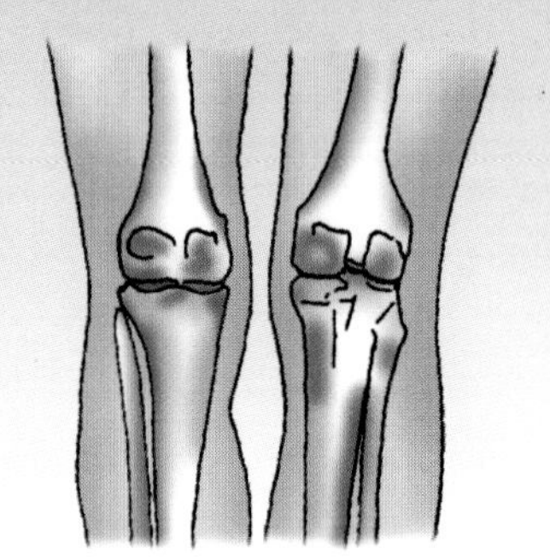

bones

ئێسك

esek

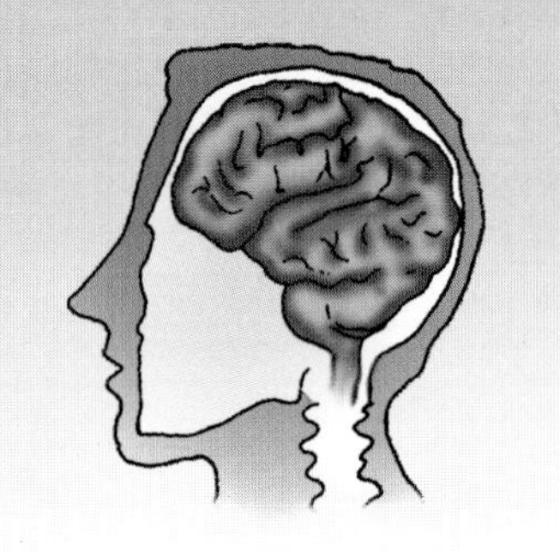

brain

مێشك

meshk

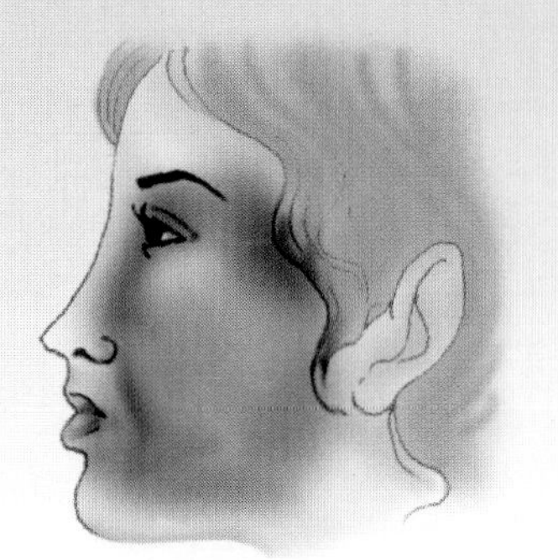

cheek

ڕوومه ت

rowmat

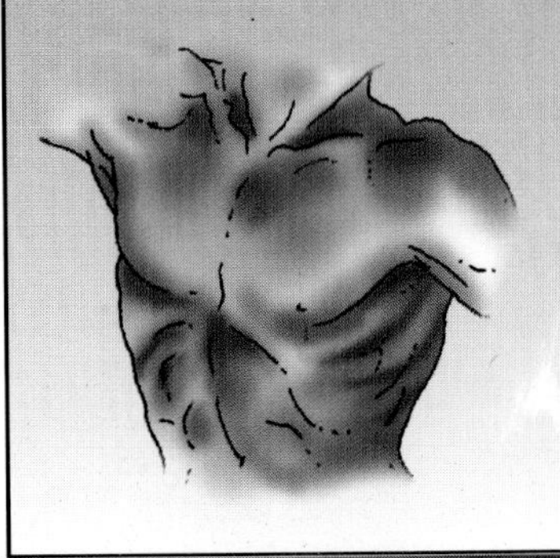

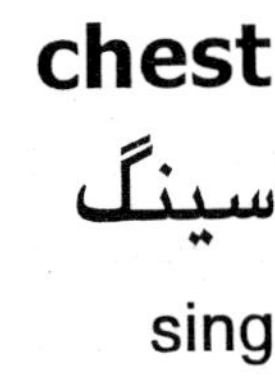

chest

سینگ

sing

chin

چه نه گه

chanaga

ear

گوێ

gouy

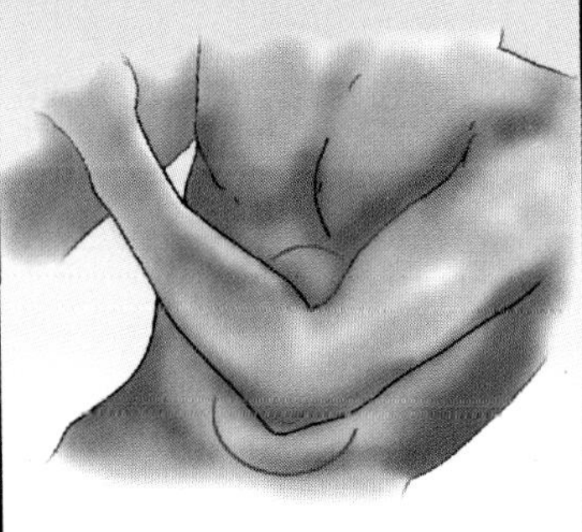

elbow

ئانیشك

anishk

eye

چاۆ

chaw

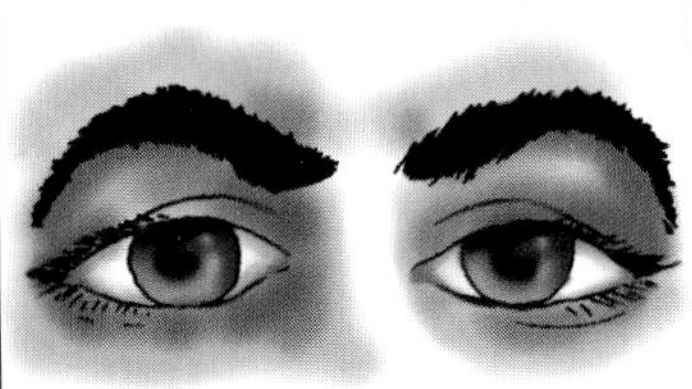

eyebrows

برۆ

brow

face

ده م و چاو

dam o chaw

fingers

قامك

ghamk

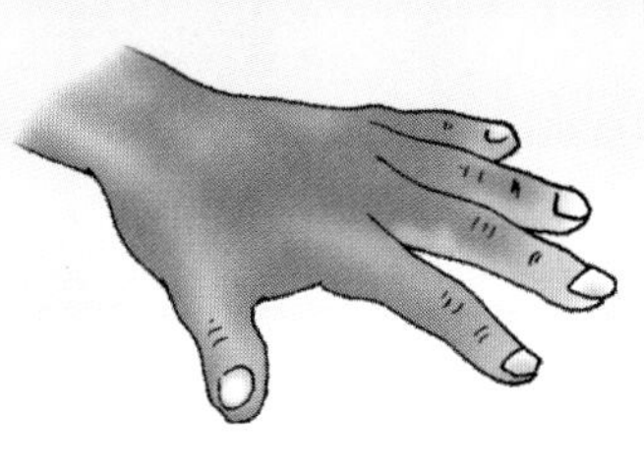

foot

پێ

pei

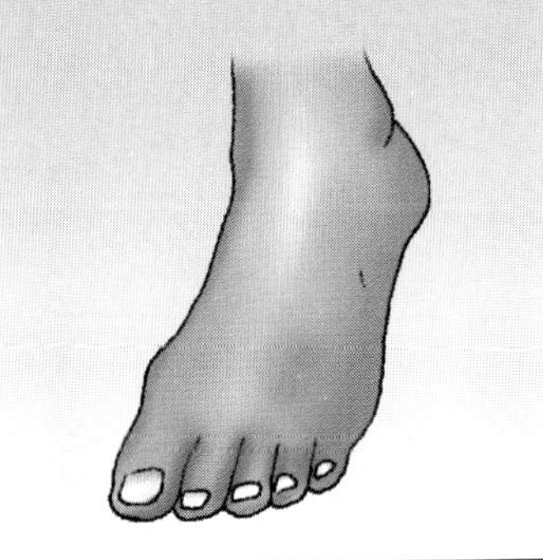

forehead

نێوچاوان

niwchawan

hair

موو

mou

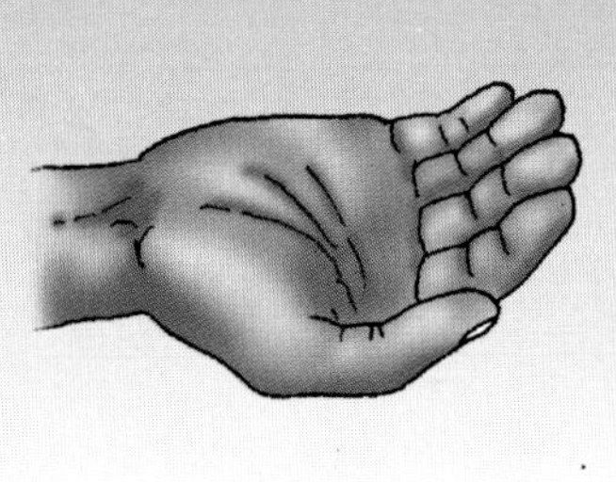

hand

ده ست

dast

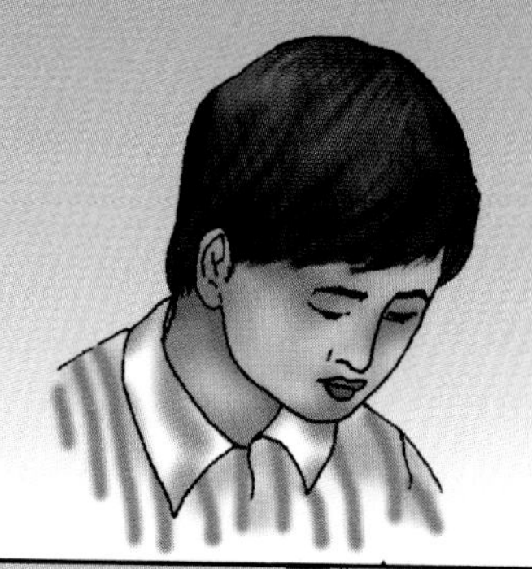

head

سه ر

sar

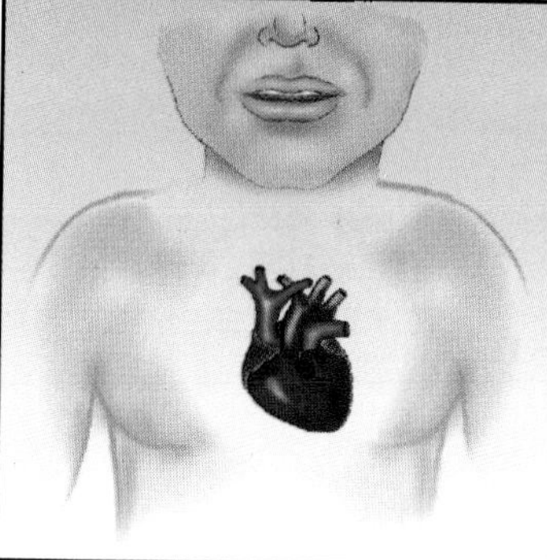

heart

دڵ

del

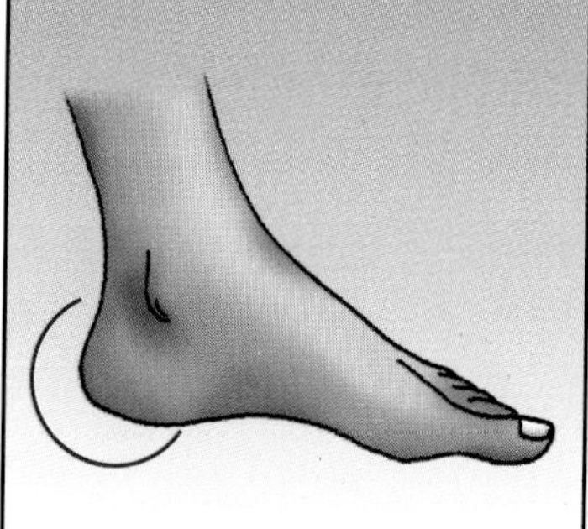

heel

پانێ

pany

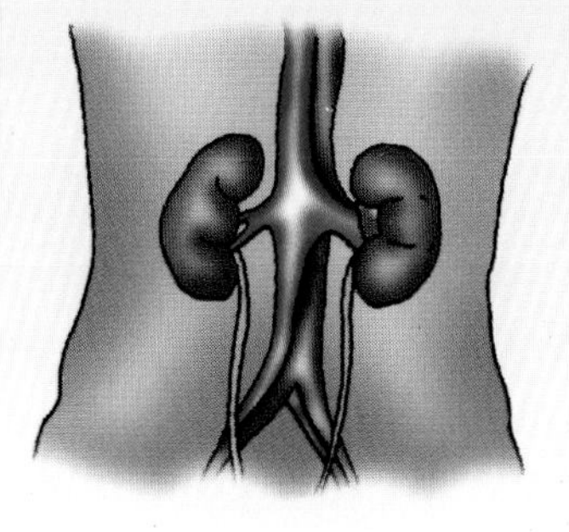

kidneys

گورچێله

gorchila

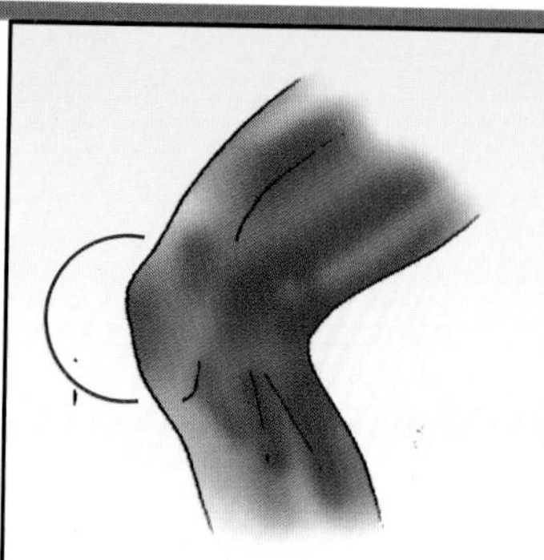

knee

ئه ژنۆ

ajhnoo

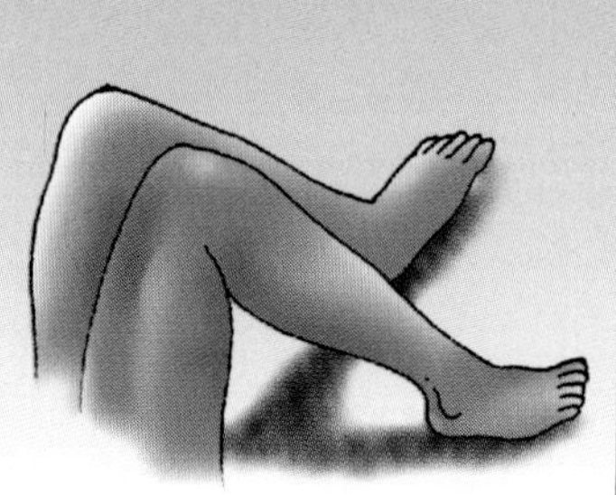

legs

لاق

lagh

lips

لێو

lew

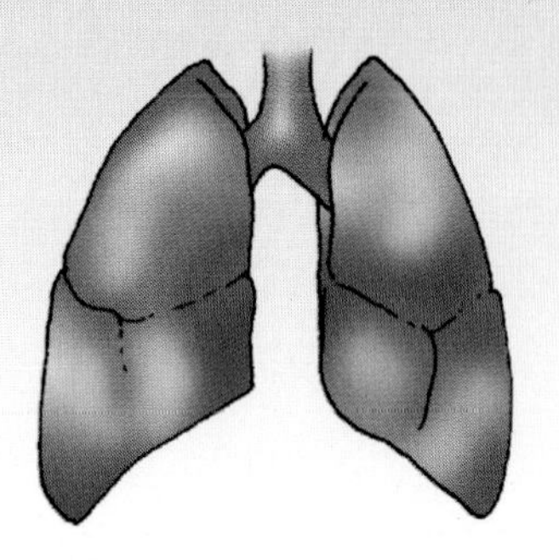

lungs

سيپه لاك

sipalak

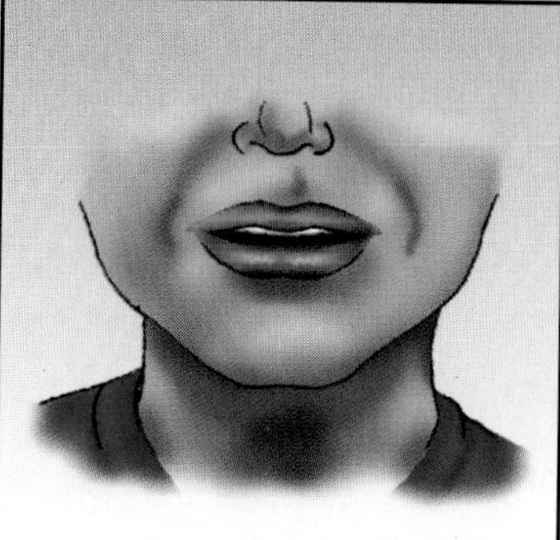

mouth

ده م–زار

dam-zar

moustache

سمێل

semel

muscle

مایچه

maicha

nails

نینۆك

ninouk

neck

مل

mel

nose

كه پۆ

kapouw

palm

له پی ده ست

lapeidast

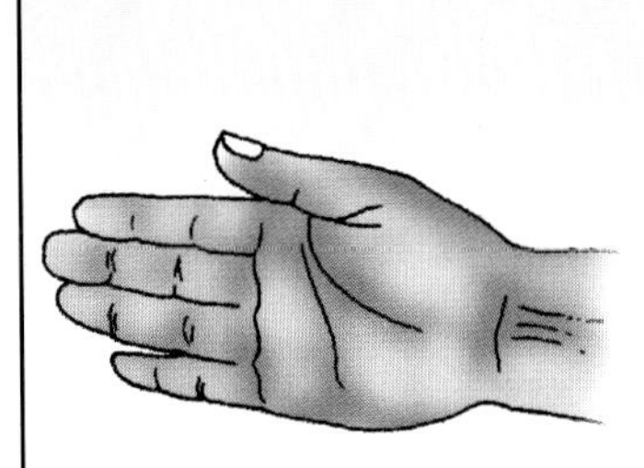

ribs

په راسوو

parasou

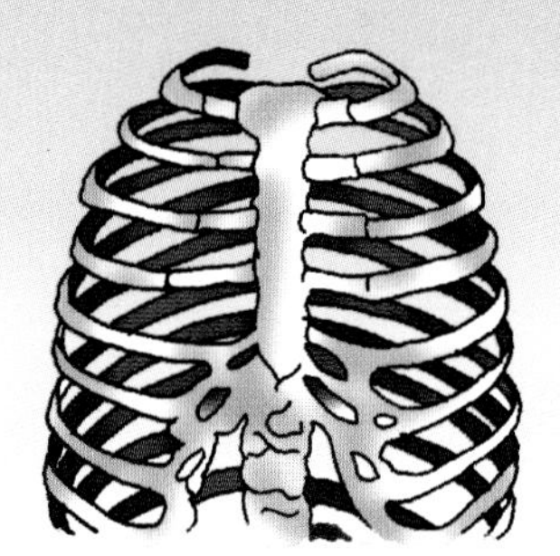

shoulders

شان

shan

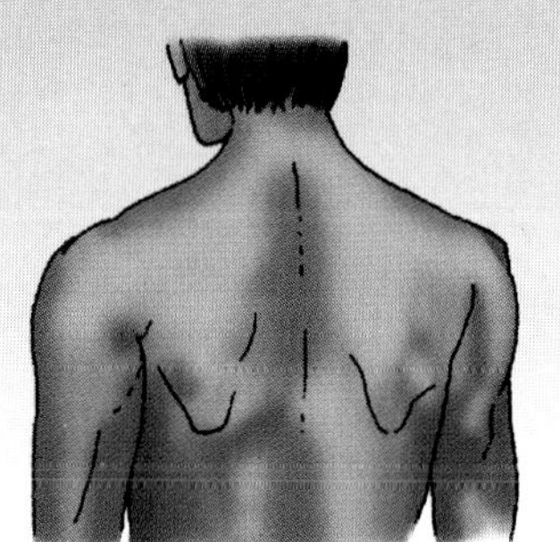

skeleton

ئێسكلیت

eskelit

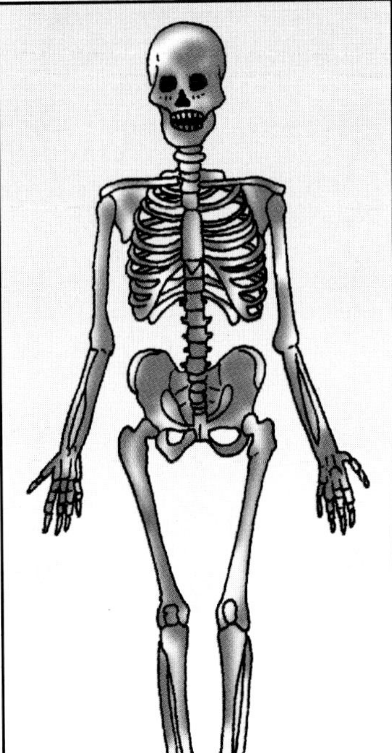

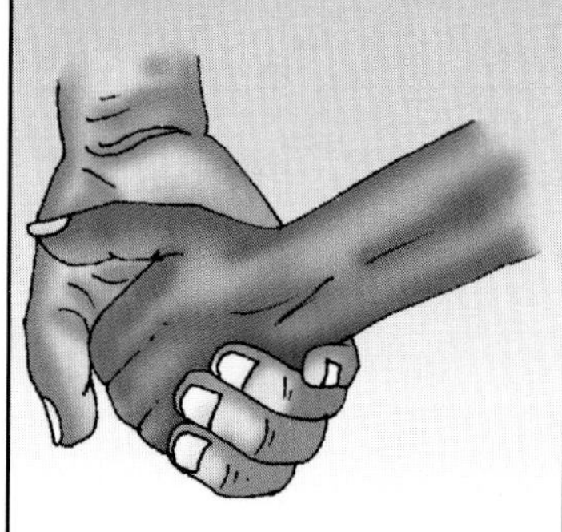

skin
پێست
pest

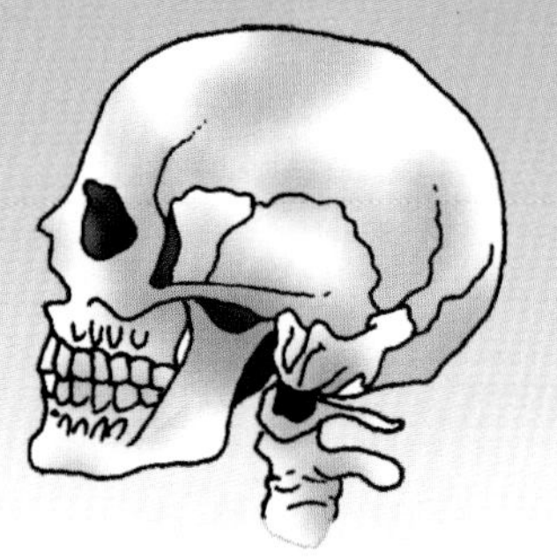

skull
که سه ی سه ر
kallei sar

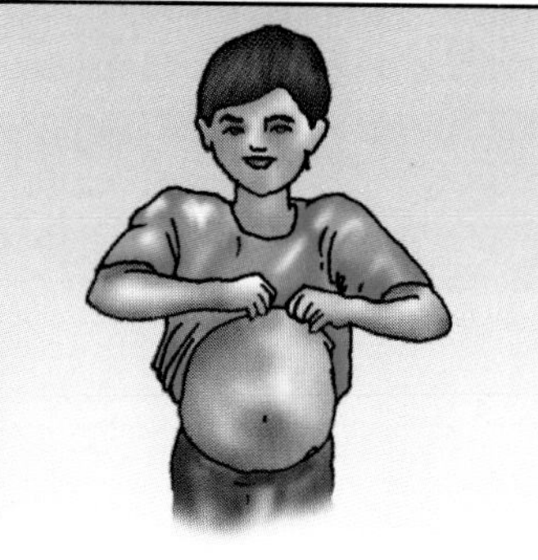

stomach
ورگ
worg

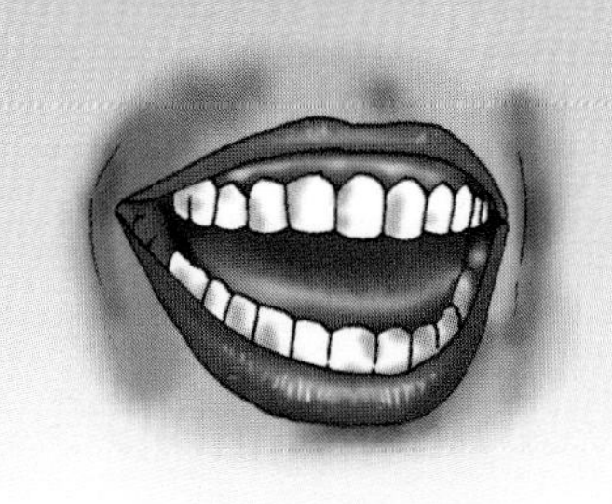

teeth
ددان
dadan

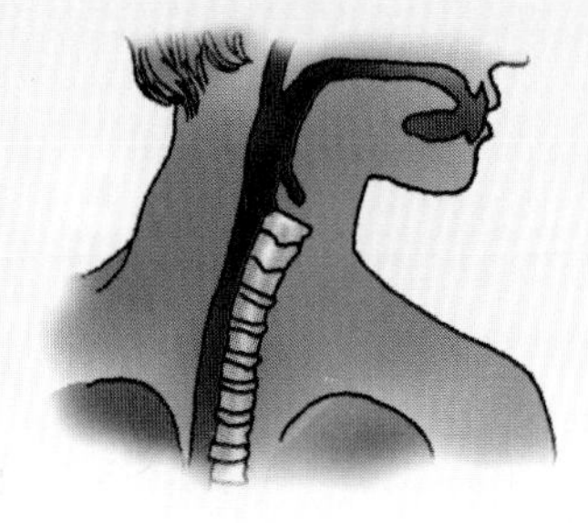

throat
گه روو
garouw

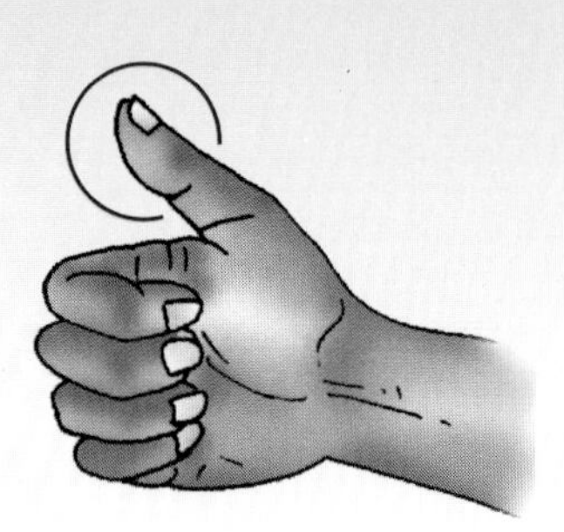

thumb
قامکی گه وره
ی ده ست
ghamki gorey dast

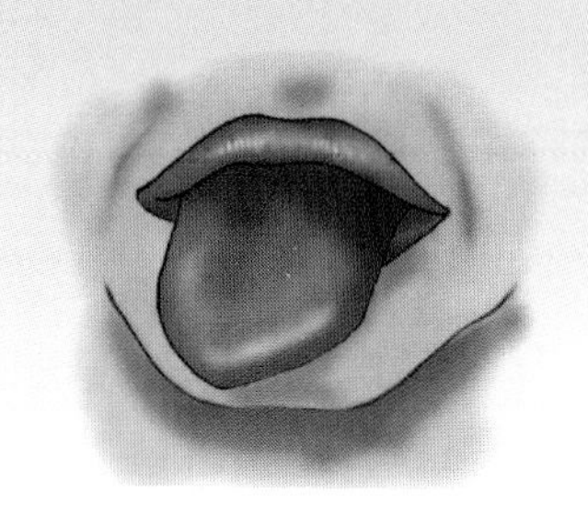

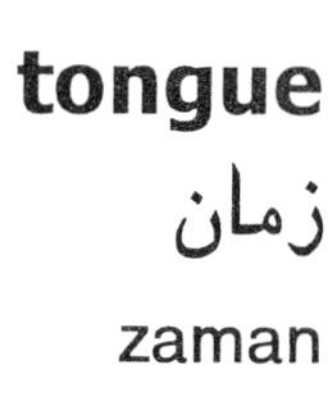

tongue
زمان
zaman

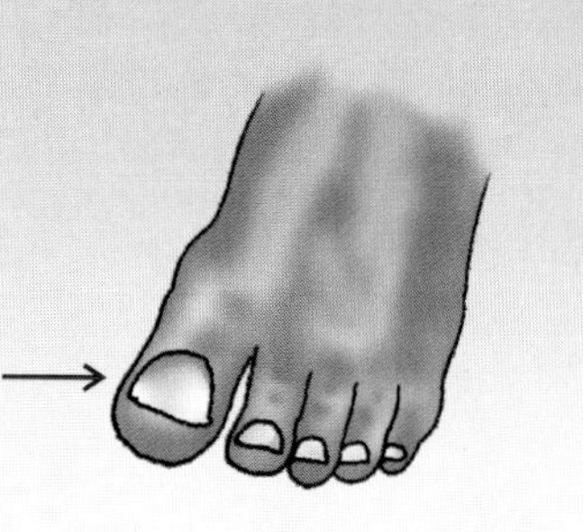

toes
قامکی لاق
ghamki lagh

waist
که مه ر
kamar

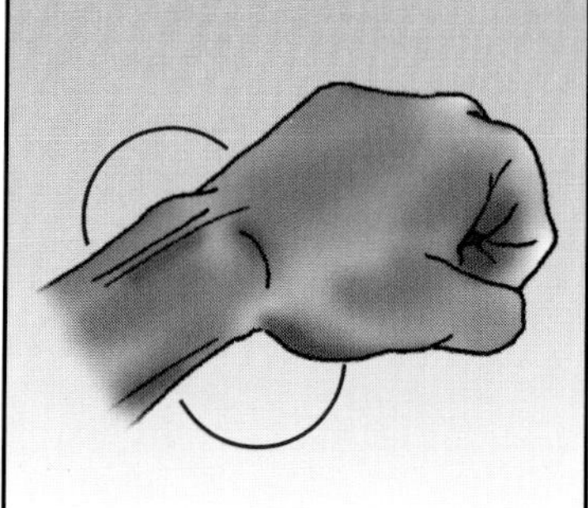

wrist
مه چه ك
machak

MEASUREMENTS, SHAPES, COLOURS AND TIME

ئه ندازه گرتن ، شكل ، ره نگ وكات

Andaza Gartan, Shakl, Rang Wakat

black

ڕە ش

rash

blue

ئاوی

avi

brown

قاوە ئی

ghaweie

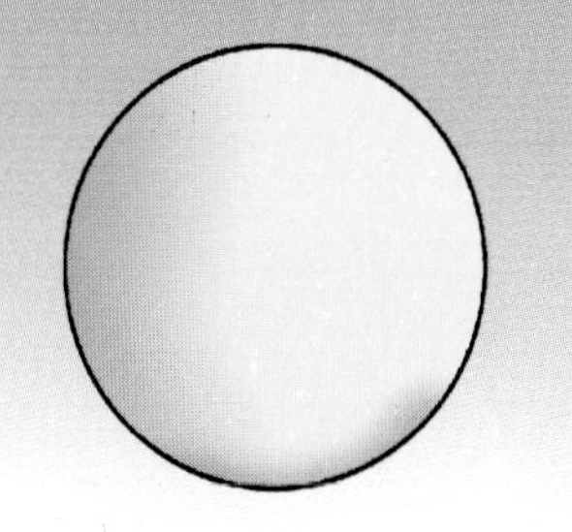

circle

دایرە

dayera

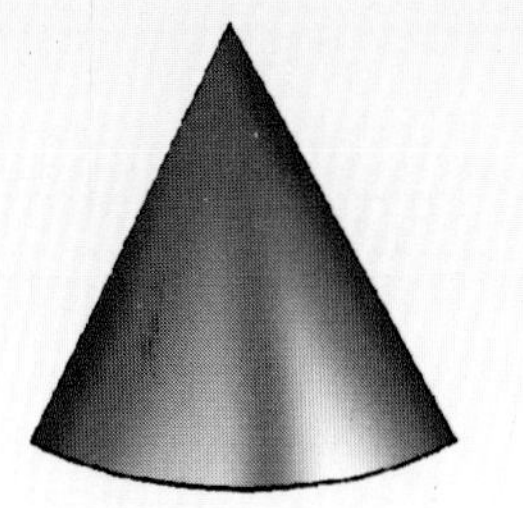

cone

مە خروت

makhrout

cube

شە ش پاڵوو

shashpalou

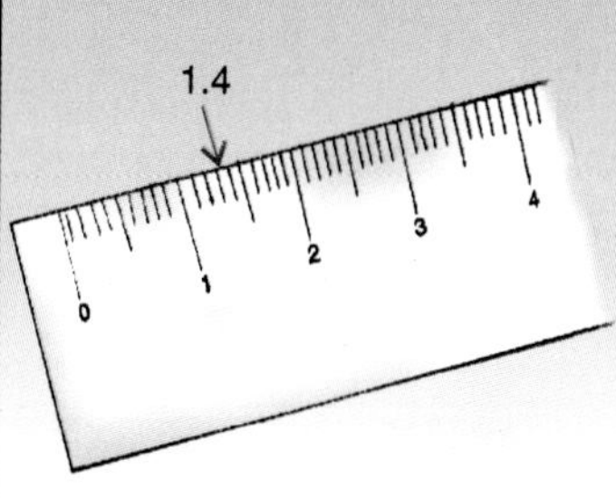

decimals

دە ئی

daie

green

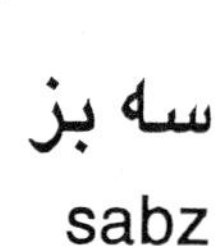

سە بز

sabz

heap

کە لە کە

kalaka

kilogram

کیلۆگرم

kilogram

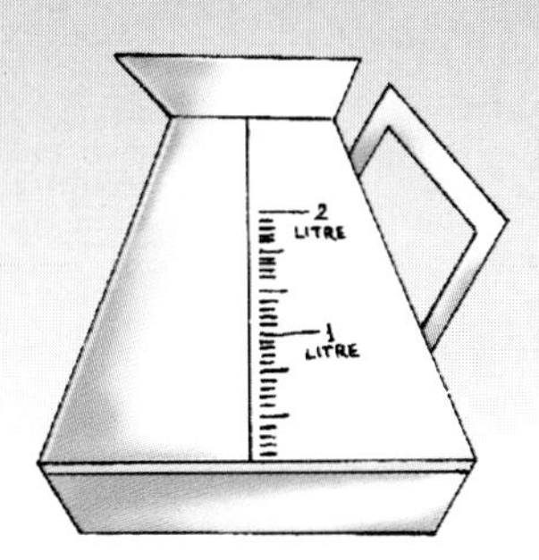

litre

ليتر

litr

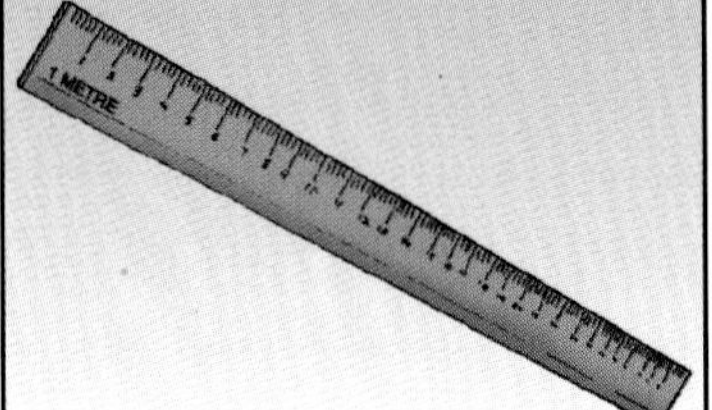

metre

متر

metr

mile

مايٚل

mile

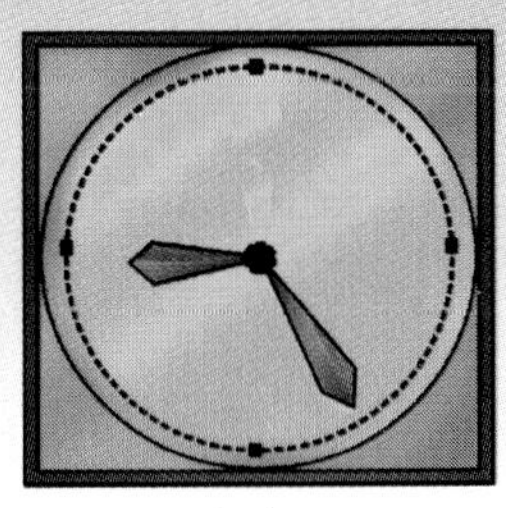

8:25

minute

ده قيقه

daghigha

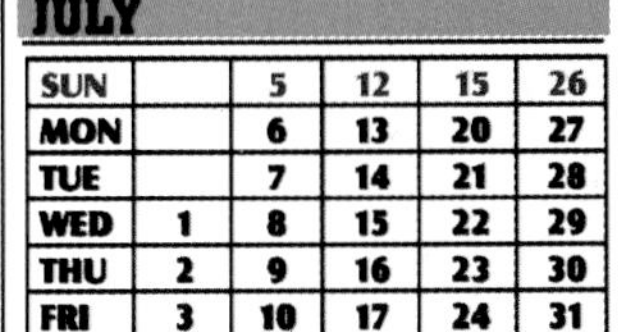

JULY

SUN		5	12	15	26
MON		6	13	20	27
TUE		7	14	21	28
WED	1	8	15	22	29
THU	2	9	16	23	30
FRI	3	10	17	24	31
SAT	4	11	18	25	

month

مانگ (سی رۆژ)

mang(si rojh)

oval

هيٚلکه ئی

helhaei

pair

جووت

jout

pink

سوره تی

sorati

rectangle

مستتيل

mostatil

red

سوور

sour

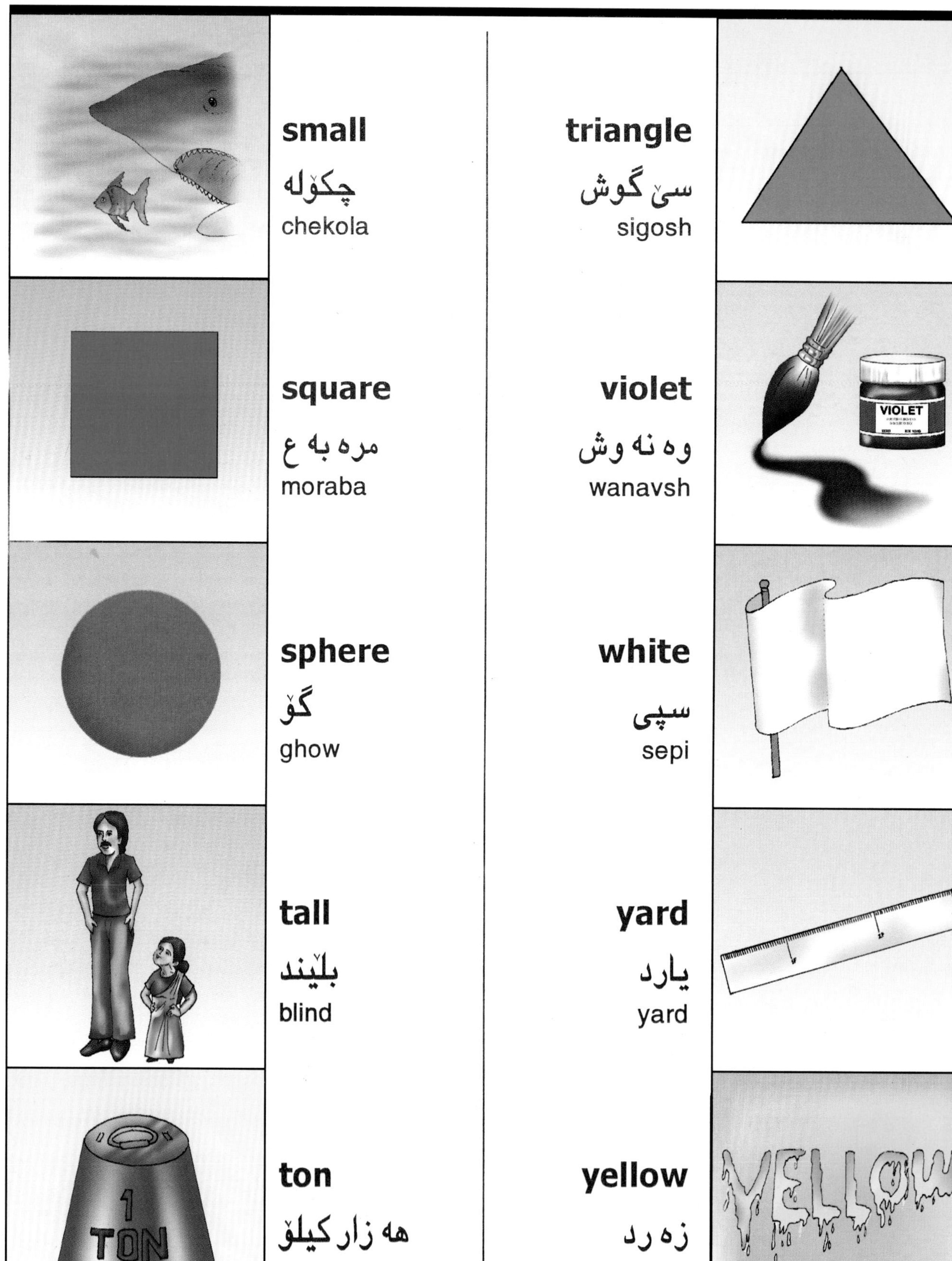

small
چكۆله
chekola

square
مره به ع
moraba

sphere
گۆ
ghow

tall
بلێند
blind

ton
هه زار كيلۆ
hazarkilo

triangle
سێ گوش
sigosh

violet
وه نه وش
wanavsh

white
سپی
sepi

yard
يارد
yard

yellow
زه رد
zard

PEOPLE, COSTUMES AND ORNAMENTS

مرۆڤ ، رە وشت وئاکار ، رازانە وە کان

Maroof, Rahwasht O Akar, Razana Wakan

actor

هونه رپیێشه ی پیاو

honarpishei piew

actress

هونه رپیێشه ی ژن

honarpishei jhen

angel

فریشته

ferishta

architect

مه عمار

mamar

artist

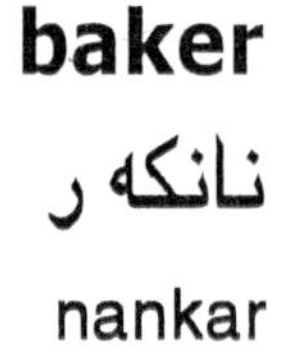

هونه ر مه ند

honarmand

astronaut

ئاسمان گه ر

asmangar

athlete

وه رزش کار

warzeshkar

author

نووسه ر

nousar

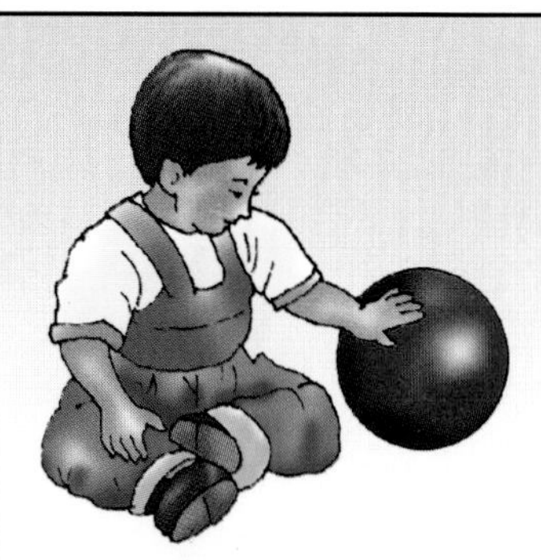

baby

منداڵ

mendal

baker

نانکه ر

nankar

bandit

دزی مسله ح

dezi mosalah

bishop

ئسقف

osghof

blacksmith

ئاسن گه ر

asengar

blouse

کراسی ژنانه

kerasi jhenana

boy

کور

kour

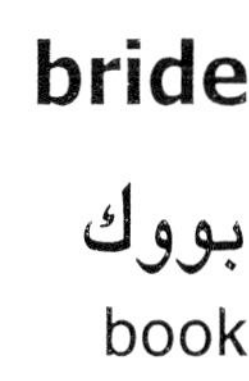

bride

بووك

book

bridegroom

زاوا

zawa

captain

کاپیتان

kapitan

caps

کلاوی ته پله

kolavi tapla

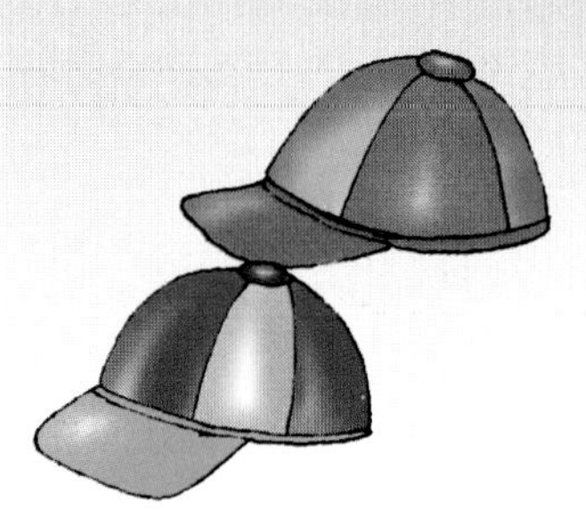

carpenter

دارتاش

dartash

child
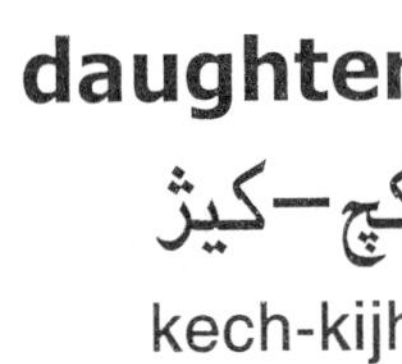
منداڵ
mendal

clown
گاڵته چی
galtachi

conductor
رێ نما
rinema

cook/chef
چێشت لی نه ر
chesht lei nar

dancers
سه ماركه ر
samakar

daughter
كچ–كيژ
kech-kijh

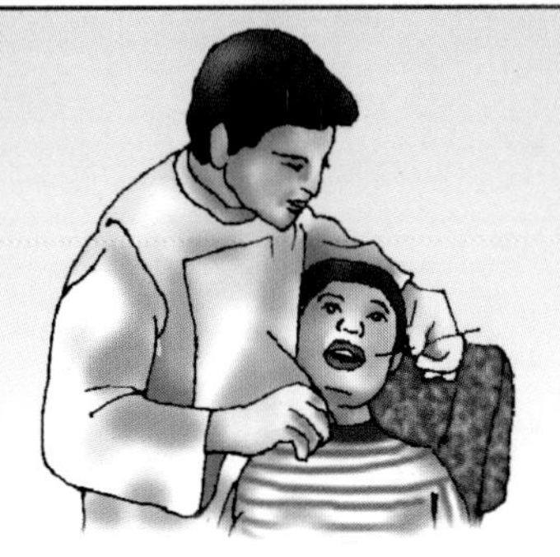

dentist
درانساز
dedansaz

doctor
دۆكتۆر
duktour

driver
رانه نده
rananda

dwarfs
چاڵاو هه ڵقه ن
chalaw halghan

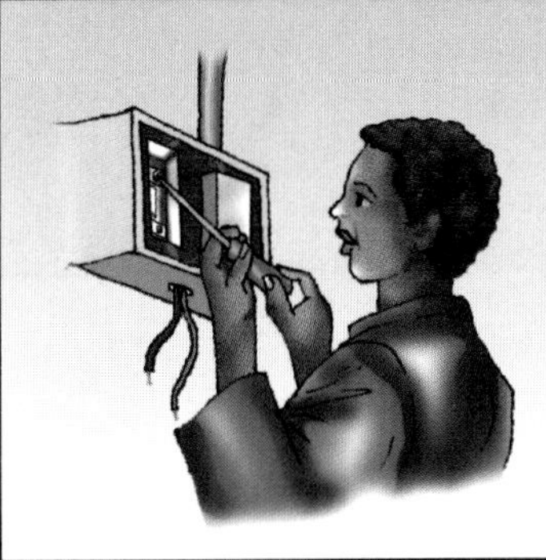

electrician

برق کار

bargh kar

farmer

جوتێر

joter

fire-fighter

ئاتش نيشان

ateshneshan

girl

کچ

kech

jacket

ژاکه ت

jhakat

king

شاه

shah

knight

شواليه

showalia

lady

خاتوون

khatoon

man

مرۆف

merouf

mechanic

مه كانيك

makanik

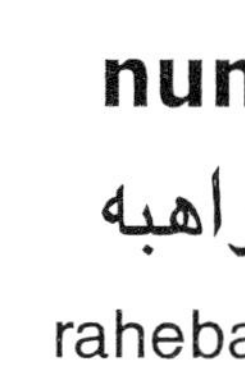

miner

مه عده ن چی

madan chi

merchant

تاجر

tajer

monk

راهب

raheb

musicians

موسیٔقی زان

mosighi zan

necktie

کراوٚات

kerawat

nun

راهبه

raheba

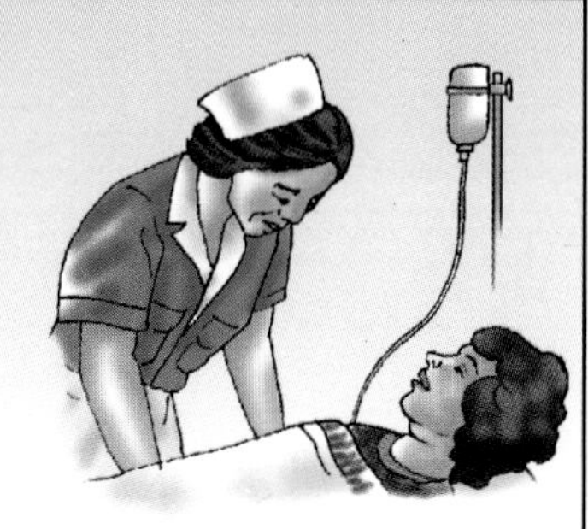

nurse

په ره ستار

parastar

painter

نگار گه ر

negargar

pilot

فروکه وان

ferukawan

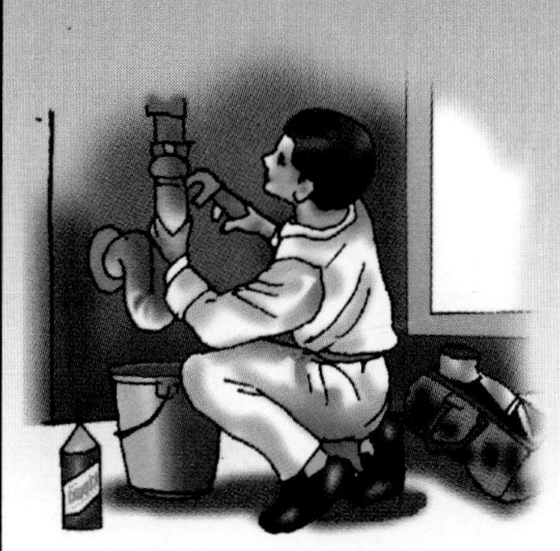

plumber

لوله کیٚش

lolakesh

police officer

ئێزگه ی پولیس

izgai polis

porter

بار به ر

barba'r

postman

پست چی

postchi

priest

قه شه

ghasha

prince

شازاده

shazadah

queen

مه له که

malaka

robber

دز

dez

sailor

مه له وان

malawan

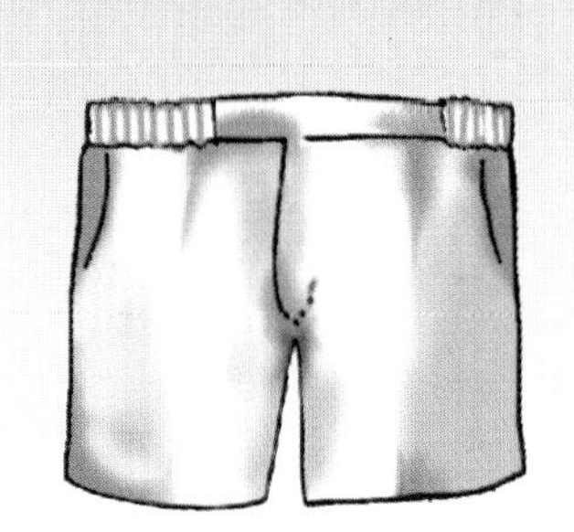

shorts

شۆرت

short

shopkeeper

دوکاندار

dowkandar

sisters
خوشك
khoshek

soldier
سه ر باز
sarbaz

solicitor
وه كيل
wakil

teacher
ماموٚستا
mamosta

thief
دزيح ماڵـان
dezi malan

turban
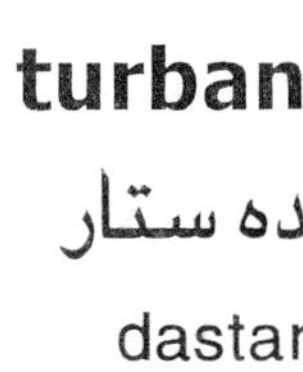
ده ستار
dastar

waiter
خزمه تكار
khezmatkar

wife
خێزان
khezan

woman
ژن
jhen

wrestlers
پاڵه وان
palawan

PLACES AND BUILDINGS

حبێ کاکان و به ناکان

Al-Amaakan Wa Al-Mubaani

airport

فرۆکه خانه

ferouka khana

aquarium

ئکواریۆم

aquarium

bank

بانك

bank

bay

که نداو

kandaw

bazar

بازار

bazaar

beach

که نارده ریا

kanardarya

bridge

پرد

perd

bungalow

ماڵی جه نگه ڵی

malijangaly

café

قاوه خانه

ghawa khana

canal

جۆگه

joga

castle

قه لا

ghala

cathedral

کیسای گه وره

kelesay gora

cave

غار

ghar

church

کلیسا

kelesa

cinema

سینه ما

sinama

circus

سیرك

sirk

clinic

ده رمانگا

darmanga

coast

كه نارده ریا

kanardarya

college

قووتابخانه

ghotabkhana

cottage

مالی یه یلاقی

mali yaylaghi

court
دادگا
dadga

den
غار
ghar

desert
بیابان
biaban

dome
گومبه ز
gombaz

factory
کارخانه
karkhana

farm
مه زرا
mazra

apartment
ئاپارتمان
aparteman

forest
جه نگه ڵ
jangal

fort
قه ڵا
ghala

gallery
داڵان
dalan

petrol station
پومپی به نزین
pompi banzin

garden
باخ
bakh

glacier
چومی سه هوٚلی
chomisaholi

gulf
که نداو
kandaw

hills
ته په
tapa

hospital
نه خوشخانه
nakhoushkhana

hostel
می وانخانه
miwankhana

hotel
هوتیٚل
hotil

house
مالٚ
mal

hut
کوٚخ
koukh

inn

ماڵی گه وره

mali gawra

island

دۆرگه

dourga

laboratory

ئه زموونگه

azmoonga

lake

چۆم

chom

lane

ڕاڕه ۆ

rarow

library

پرتوك خانه

partook khana

light house

فانووسی دریائی

fanousi daryaie

market

بازار

bazar

monument

كۆته ڵ

kotal

mosque

مزگه وت

mezgawt

mountain
کێو–چیا
kiw-chia

museum
مووزه
moza

observatory
رهسه دخانه
rasadhana

ocean
ئوقیانووس
oghyanus

office
ده فتری کار
daftari kar

orchard
زه مێنی که
داری مێوه ی به
zamini ke dari
mivei be

palace
کۆشك
koshk

park
پارك
park

pavement
پیاده رو
piadarow

pillars
کۆڵه که
kowlaka

play ground
مه یدانی یاری
maydani yari

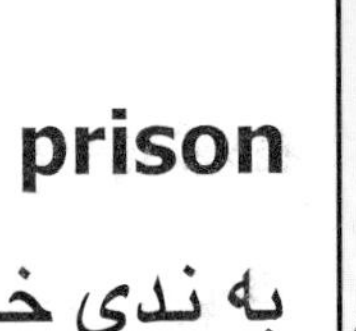

prison
به ندی خانه
bandykhana

pond
گۆل
gol

restaurant
چێست خانه
chestkhana

pool
ئسته خر
estakhr

river
ڕووبار
rowbar

port
به نده ر
bandar

road
ڕیگا
reiga

post-office

پۆستخانه
postkhana

school

قوتابخانه
ghotabkhana

workshop
جێ کار
ji kar

shop
دوکان
dowkan

skyscrapers
ماڵی زور بڵند
mali zor blind

stadium
ئستادیوم
estadiom

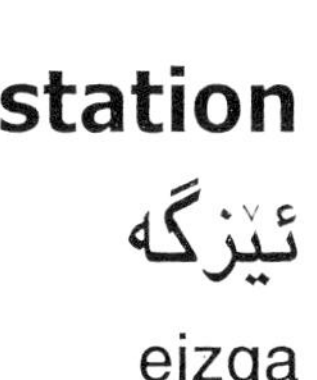

station
ئێزگه
eizga

street
شه قام
shagham

subway
راڕه ۆی ژێرئه
رزی
raroui jher arzi

supermarket
سوپرمارکت
supermaket

swimming pool
ئسته خری مه ری
estakhri marei

temple
په ره سگه
parasga

theatre
تئاتر
teatr

tower
بورج
bourj

town
شار
shar

tunnel
تونێل
tounel

university
زانکۆ
zankow

valley
دۆل–شێو
dowl-shiw

village
گوند
gond

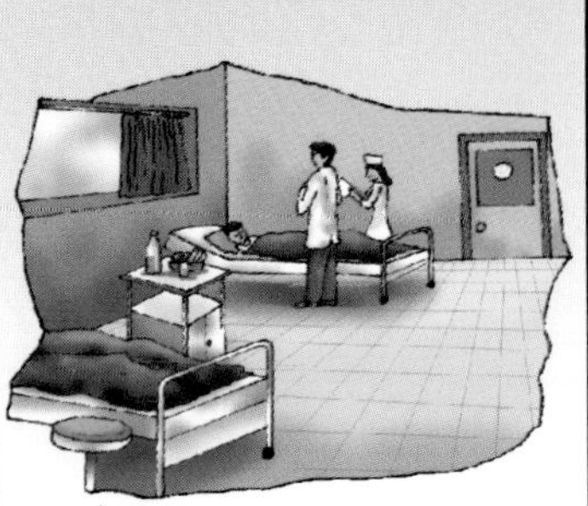

ward/clinic
ده رمانگا
darmanga

zoo
باغی وه حش
baghy vahsh

PLANTS AND FLOWERS

گووڵ و گێا

Gol O Gaya

balsam
گوڵی خه نه
guli khane

bamboo
خه یزه ران
khayzaran

branch
شاخه
shakha

bush
گوڵی پێتاڵ
guli papital

cactus
کاکتوس
kaktous

corn

سه رداری
sardary

cotton
که تان
katan

daffodil
نه رگسی زه رد
nargesy zard

dandelion
گوڵی په پوله
guli papula

eggplant
بامجانی ڕه ش
bamjany rash

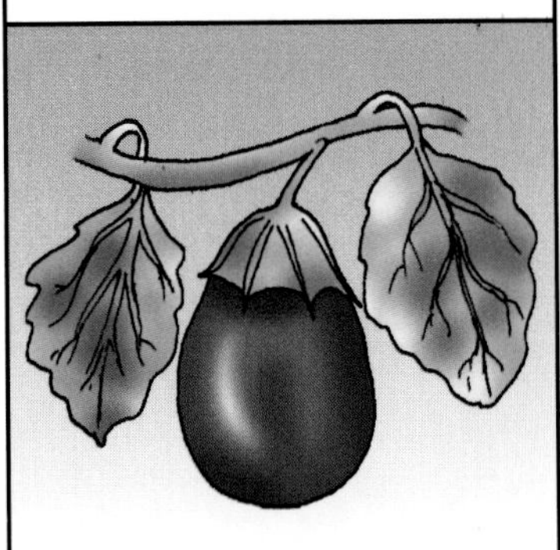

elm

داری ناروه ن

dari narvan

fir

سنه و به ر

senowba'r

flax

به زه ره ك

bazarak

grass

چه مه ن

chaman

heliopsis

جوريك گول

jorik gol

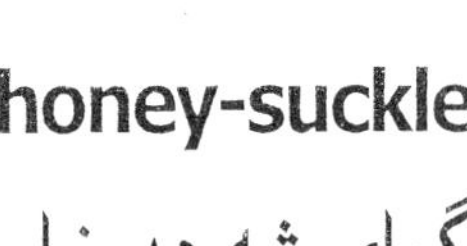

honey-suckle

گیای شه هد خار

giay shahd khar

jasmine

یاسه مه ن

yasaman

lily

سوسه نی سپی

sosany sepi

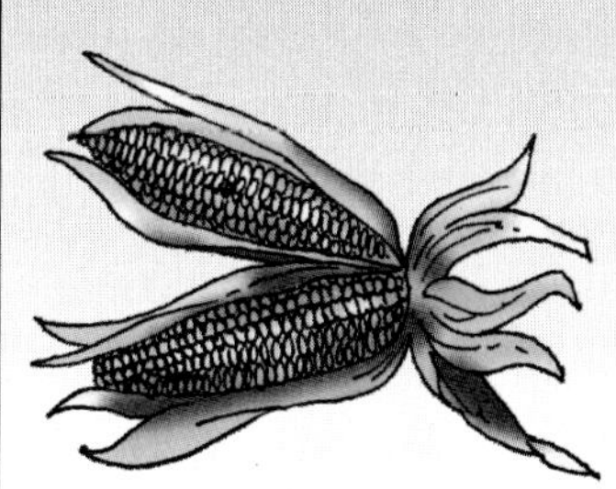

maize

سه رداری

sardary

narcissus

نه رگس

narges

olive
زه یتون
zaytoun

palm trees
داری خورما
dary khorma

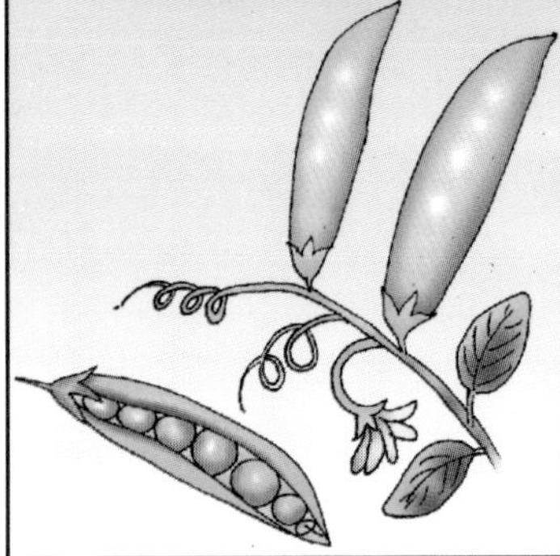

peas
نوکه فه ره نگی
nouka farangy

root
ره گ و ریشه
ragu risha

rose
گولی سوور
guli sour

sugarcanes
نه یشه که ر
nayshekar

tobacco
توتن
toten

vanilla
وانیل
wanil

water-lilies
نیلوفه ری ئاوی
nilofary avi

zinnias
گولی ئاهار
goly agar

SPORTS, GAMES AND RECREATION

وه رزش ، یاری ، گه پ و گاڵته

Warzish , Yari , Gap O Galta

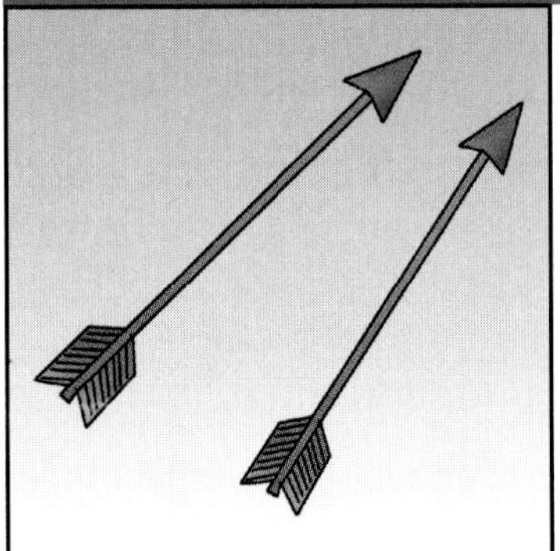

arrows

تیر

tir

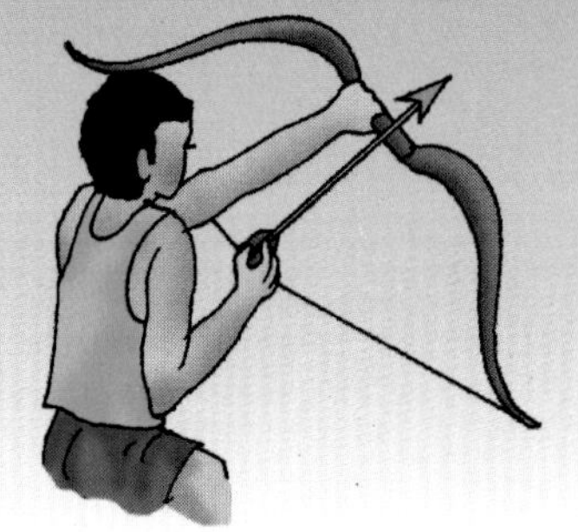

archery

تیربازی

tirbazy

badminton

به دمیٚن توٚن

badminton

ball

توٚپ

toup

balloons

بالوٚن

ballon

billiard

بیلیارد

billiard

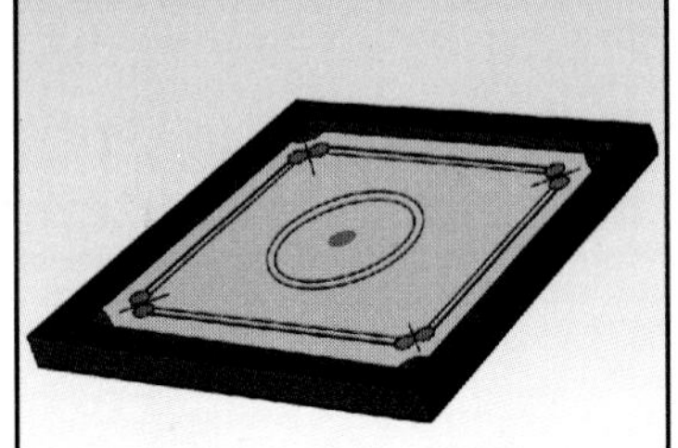

carrom board

جوره بازیٚك

jora bazeek

chess

شه تره نج

shatranj

clarinet

دووزه له

dowzala

cornet

شه یپوور

shaipour

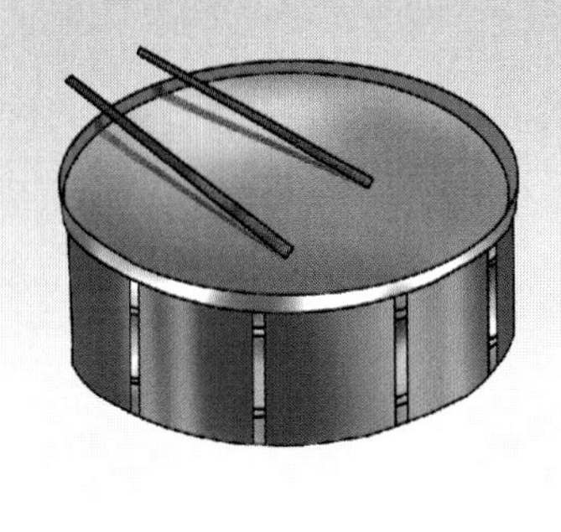

drum

ده هۆوڵ

dahoul

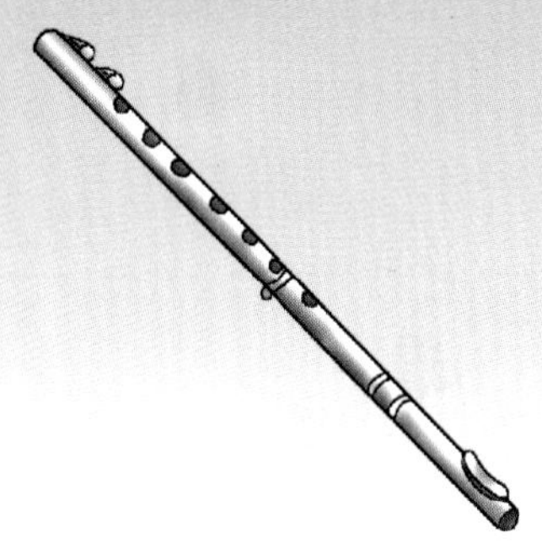

flute

دووزه له

dowzala

cricket

کریکئت

keriket

football

فوتپاڵ

fotpal

golf

گۆلف

golf

guitar

گیتار

gitar

hockey

هاکی

haky

kite

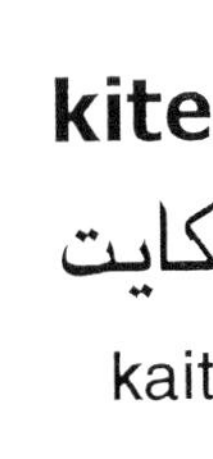

کایت

kait

mandolin

ماندولین

mandolin

puppets

بیجبێ جه ك خانم

bijbijak khanem

racket

راكێت

raket

seesaw

ئاللە دۆشە

alladosha

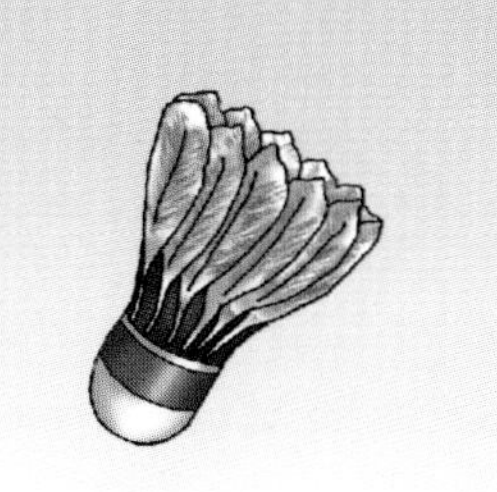

shuttle-cock

تۆپی به دمین تۆن

topy badminton

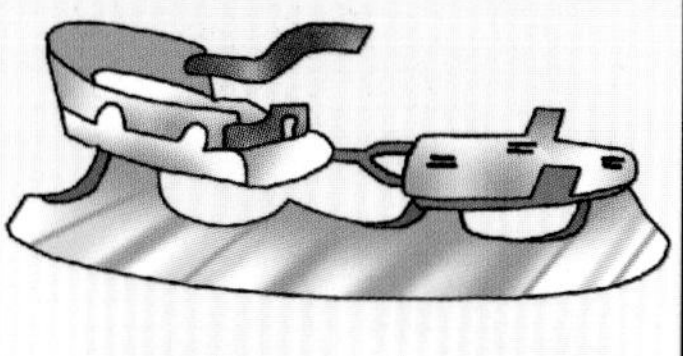

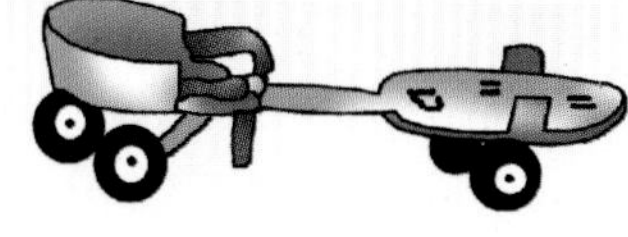

skates

ئسكێت

eskat

ski

ئسكی

iski

swing

جۆللانه

jollana

tennis

تێ نیس

tinis

trumpet

ترۆمپیێت

teroumpit

violin

ویلۆن

vielon

TRANSPORT AND COMMUNICATION

هینان و بردن ، پێو ندێکان

Henan O Bardan, Pewandekan

aeroplane
فرۆکه
ferouka

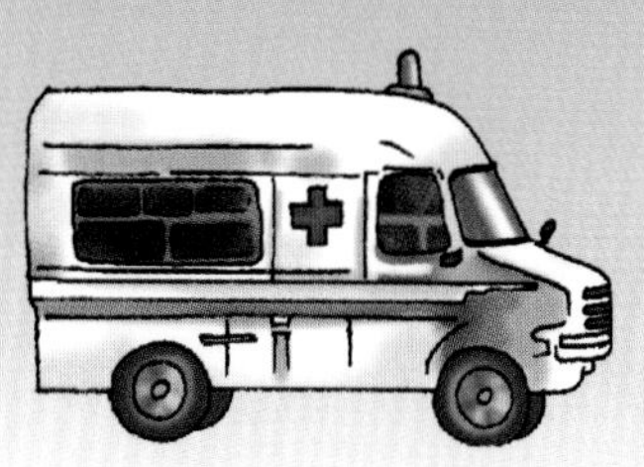

ambulance
ئامبوولانس
ambolans

automobiles
ئه و تومو بیل
avtomobyl

balloon
بالۆن
ballon

bicycle
دووچه رخه
dowcharkha

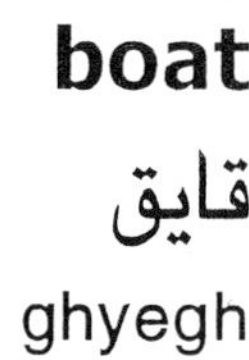

boat
قایق
ghyegh

bus
ئۆتۆبوس
aoutobus

bullock cart
گاری گای
gary gay

bull-dozer
بولدوزێر
boldozer

cable car
تلی کابین
telikabin

car

ماشین

mashen

caravan

کاراۆان

caravan

cart

چه رخی ده ستی

charkhy dasti

chariot

فایتون

fayton

coach

راهێنه ر

rahenar

crane

جه ری سه قیل

jarry saghil

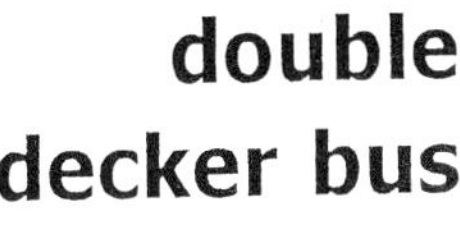

double decker bus

ئۆتۆبوس

autobus

engine (railway)

قه تار

ghatar

fax

ماشینی فاکس

mashiny faks

fire-engine

ئاته ش نێشان

atashnishan

generator
ژێنی راتۆر
jhenirator

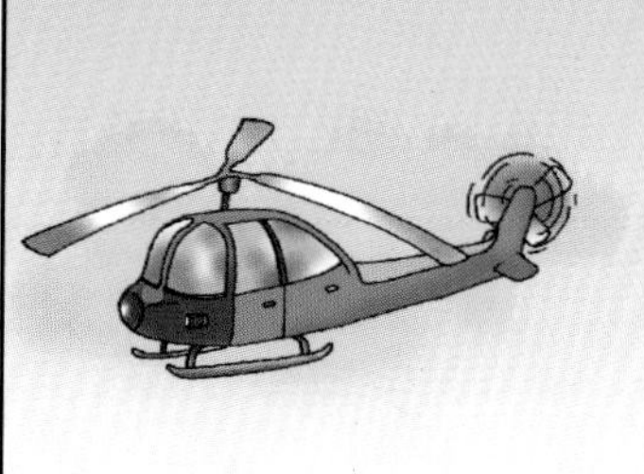

helicopter
هێلی کوپتر
hilikopter

hover-craft
هاوورکرافت
hover craft

jeep
جیپ
jeep

letter
نامه
nama

motorcycle
موتورسیکلئت
motorsyklet

parachute
چه تری ڕزگاری
chatry rezgary

petrol pumps
پۆمپی به نزین
pompy banzin

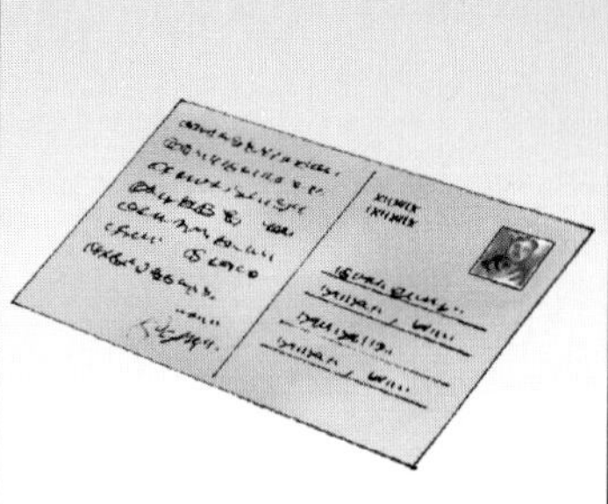

post-card
کارت پۆستال
kartopostal

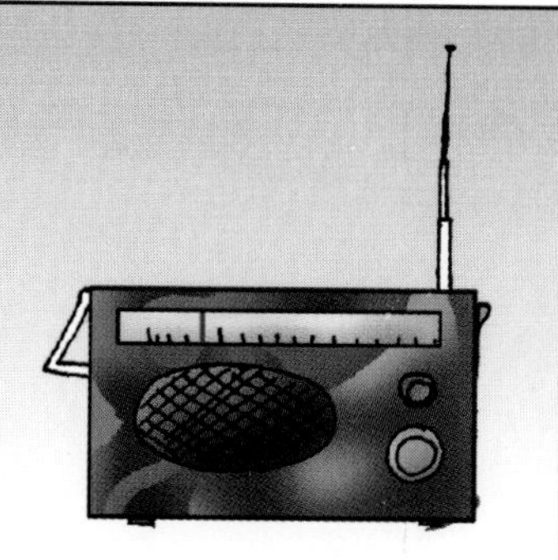

radio
رادیۆ
radiu

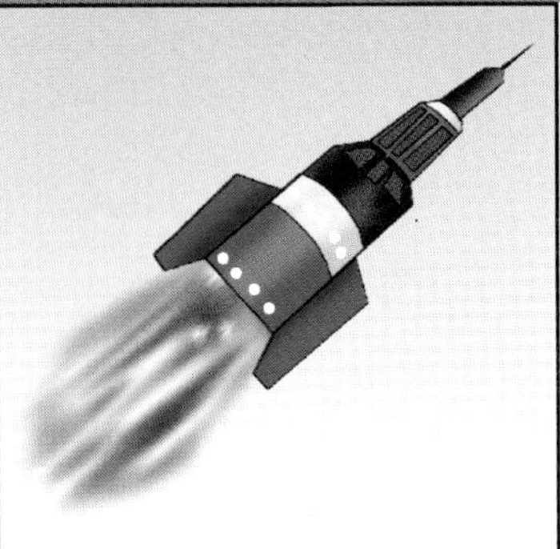

rocket

موشه ك

moshak

scooter

جوره موتور

jora motor

ship

كه شتى

kashty

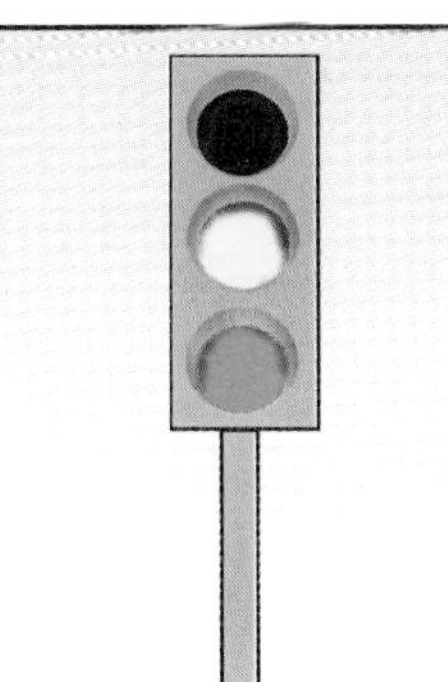

signal

نيشانه

nishana

stamp

ته مر

tamr

submarine

ژێرده ريائى

jherdaryaie

tanker

تانكێر

tankir

taxi

تاكسى

taxi

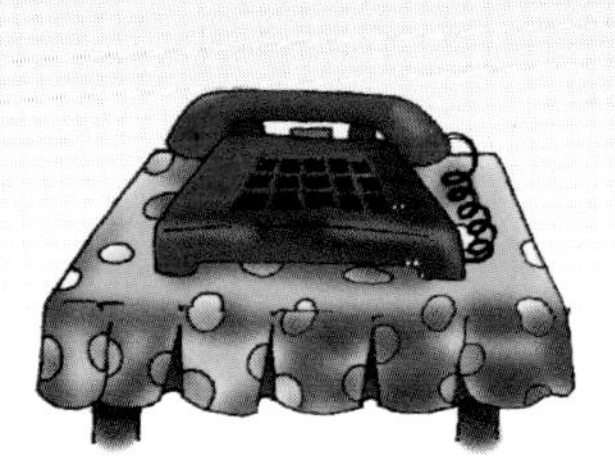

telephone

تێ لێ فۆن

tilifoun

television

تلويزون

telwizon

typewriter
ماشێنی نووسێن
mashiny nousin

tractor
تراکتۆر
teraktor

train
ترێلێ
tereily

tricycle
سێ چه رخه
si charkha

tri-shaw
سێ چه رخه
si charkha

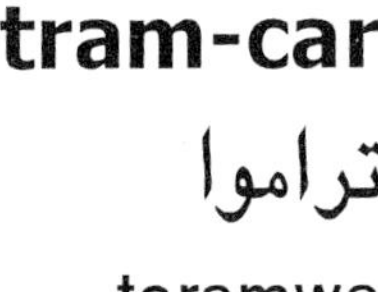

tram-car
تراموا
teramwa

van
کامیۆن
kamioun

vehicles
وه سیله ی هات
وچو
vasiley
hatochow

wheel
چه رخ
charkh

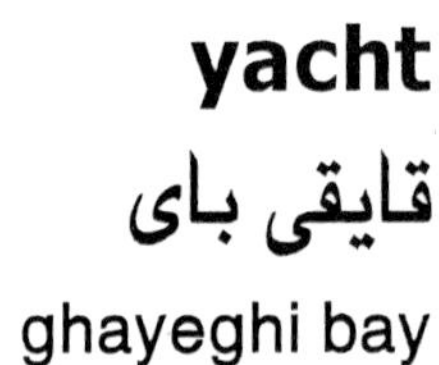

yacht
قایقی بای
ghayeghi bay

UNIVERSE AND WEATHER

جیهان و اب و هه وا

Jihan O Ab O Hawa

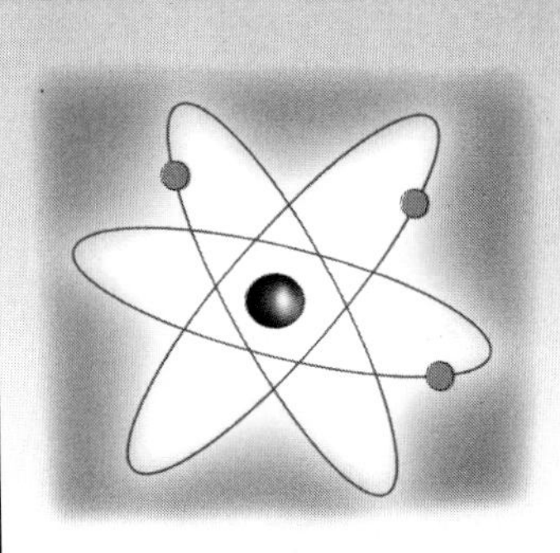

atom
ئه تۆم
atom

autumn
پائیز
paeiz

avalanche
به همه ن
bahman

blizzard
باووبۆران
bawo buran

cloud
هه ور
hawar

comet

ئه ستێره ی
کلکدار
asterey kelkdar

drought

ووشکه سالێ
woshkasali

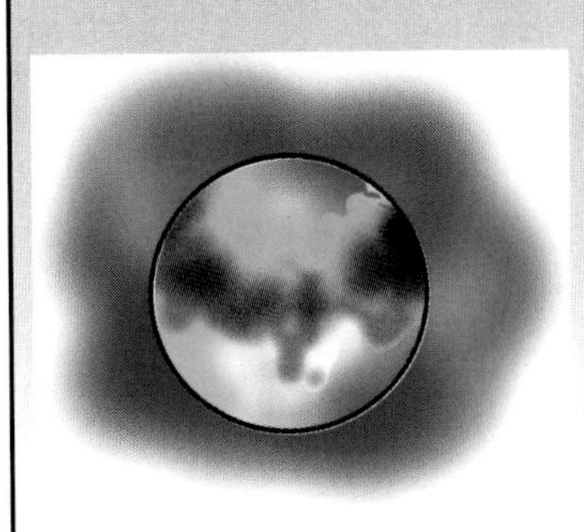

earth
ئه رز
arz

earthquake
بووله رزه
bowlarza

eclipse

خسووف
khosof

flood
سێلاو
selaw

fog
مژ
mejh

globe
كوره ى ئه رزى
korey arzy

lightning
هه وروبروسكه
hawr o broska

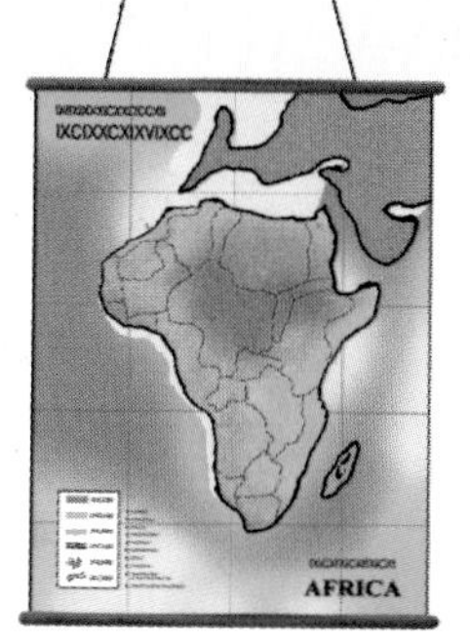

map
نه خشه
nakhsha

orbit
مه دار
madar

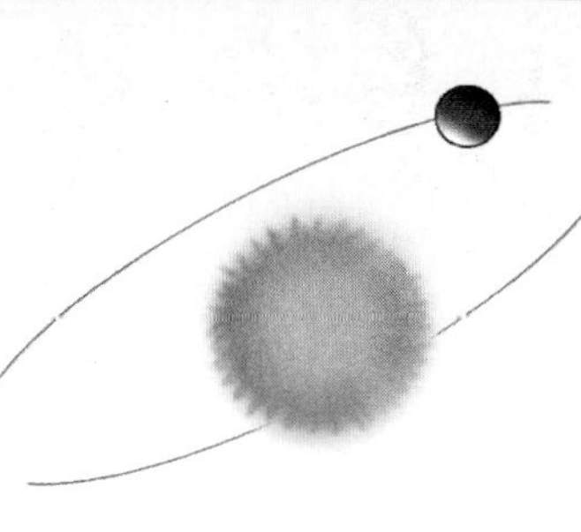

rain
واران
waran

satellite
ماهواره
mahwara

sky
ئاسمان
aseman

snow
به فر
bafr

space

فه زا

faza

spring

به هار

bahar

storm

توفان

towfan

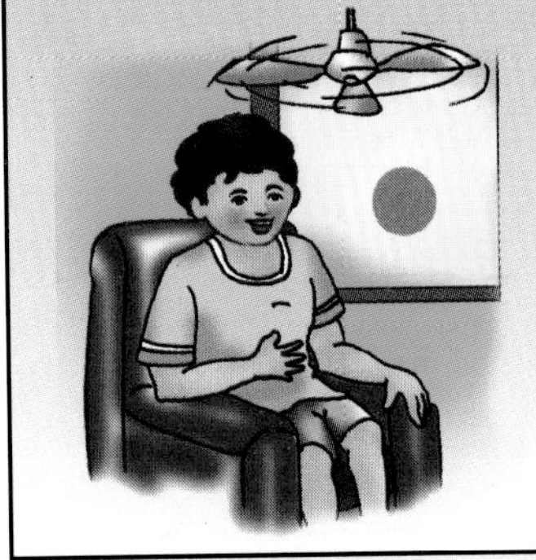

summer

هاوین

hawin

sun

رۆژ

rowjh

thunder

هه وره گه رمه

hawragarma

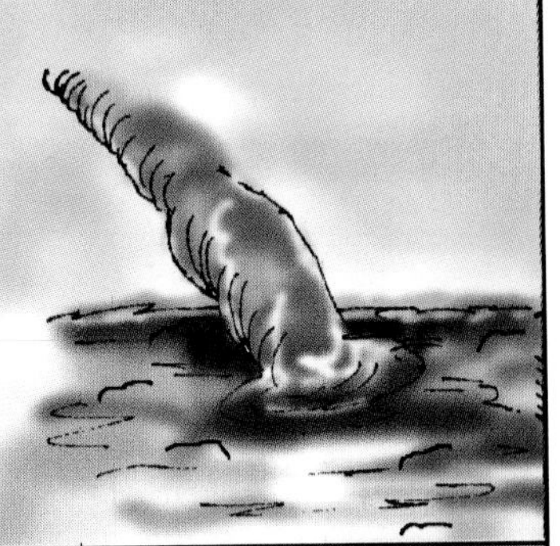

tornado

گێژه ڵووکه

gijhaloka

typhoon

توفان

towfan

volcano

ئه ته ش فشان

atashfeshan

winter

زستان

zestan

OTHER USEFUL WORDS

دووشه كانى قازانجى تر

Dosha Kani Ghazanji Tar

album
ئالبوم
album

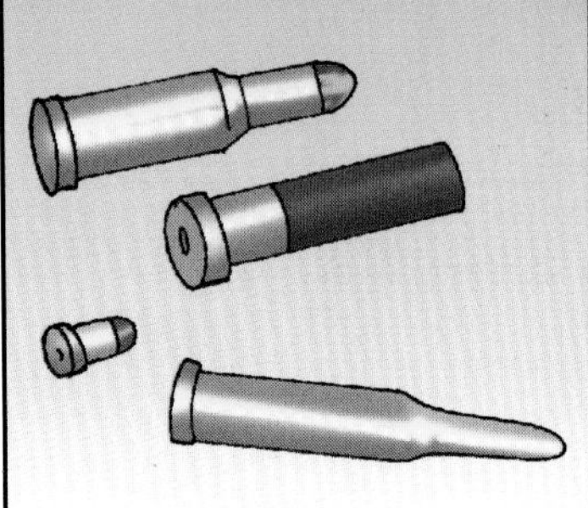

ammunition
بارۆت
barot

axe
ته وه ر
tawar

badges
پێناس
pinas

bags
کیف
kif

barrel

بۆسکه
boska

baskets
قهرتاڵه
ghartala

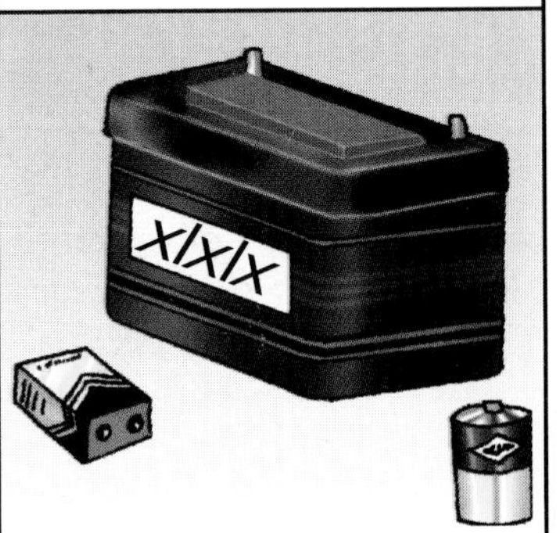

batteries

باتری
batry

bells
زه نگ
zang

book

کتێب
ketib

bottles

بوتری

botry

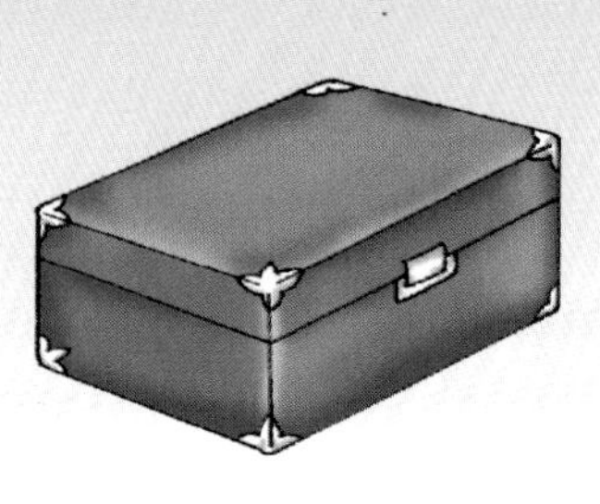

box

جه عبه

jaba

bricks

ئاجور

ajour

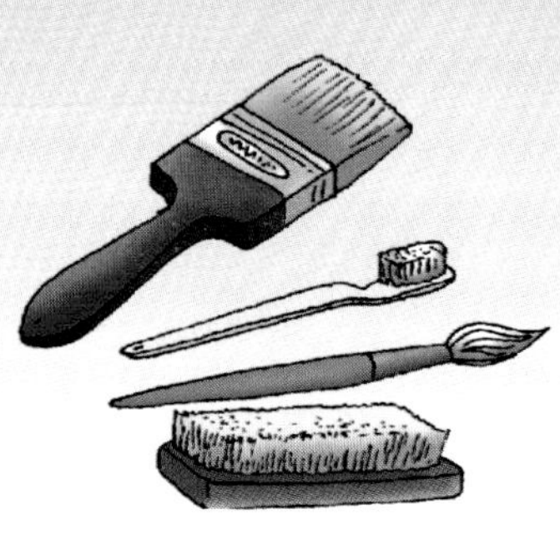

brushes

بروس

brous

belt

پشتێند

peshtend

buttons

دوگمه

dogma

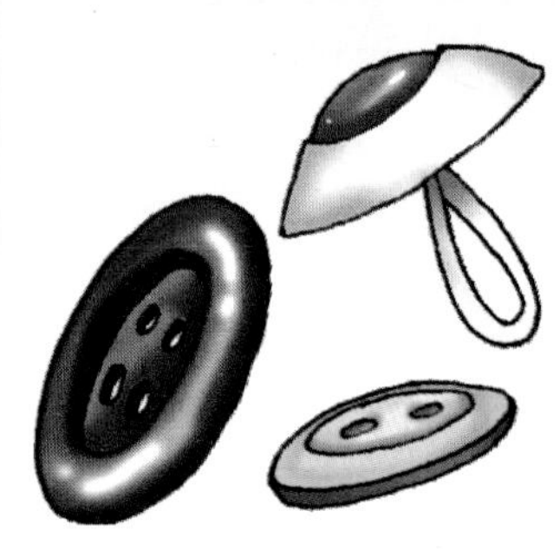

cable

سیم

sim

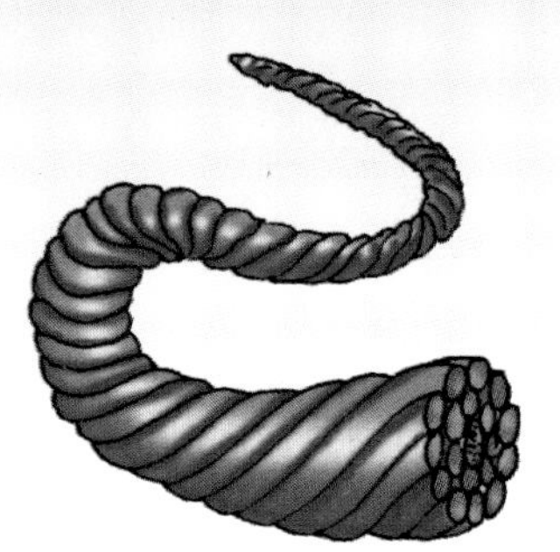

cage

قه فه س

ghafas

camera

دوربین

dourbin

candle

شه م

sham

playing cards
کارتی یاری
karty yari

chain
زه نجیر
zanjir

cheque
چه ك
chak

clock
کات ئه ژمێر
katajhmir

coal
ڕه ژی
rajhy

coins
قه ره پووڵ
ghara pool

combs
شانه
shana

computer
راێانه
rayana

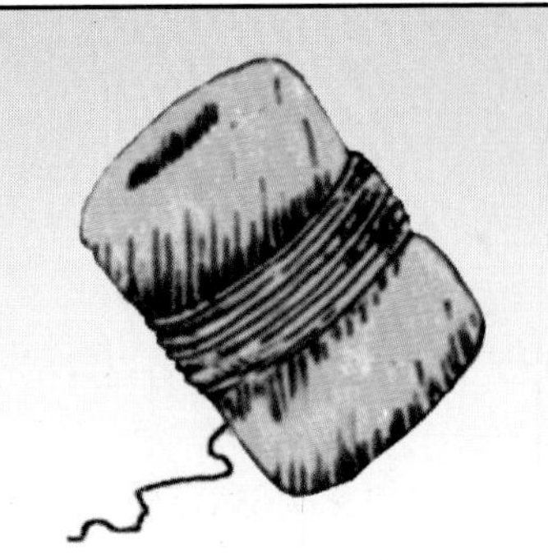

cord
ته ناف
tanaf

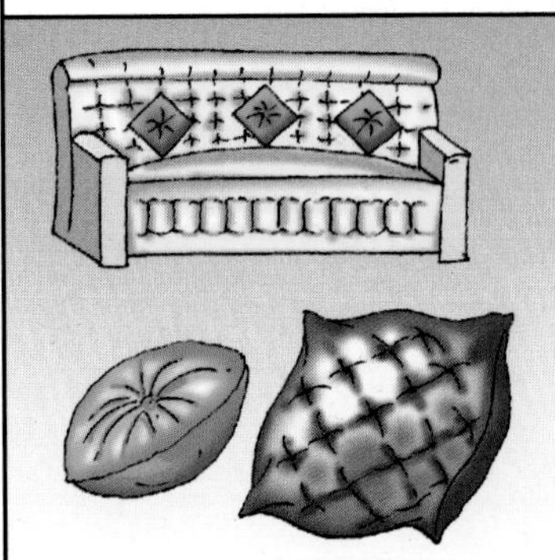

cushions
باڵنج
balenj

cylinder

سیله ندر

silandr

dagger

خه نجه ر

khanjar

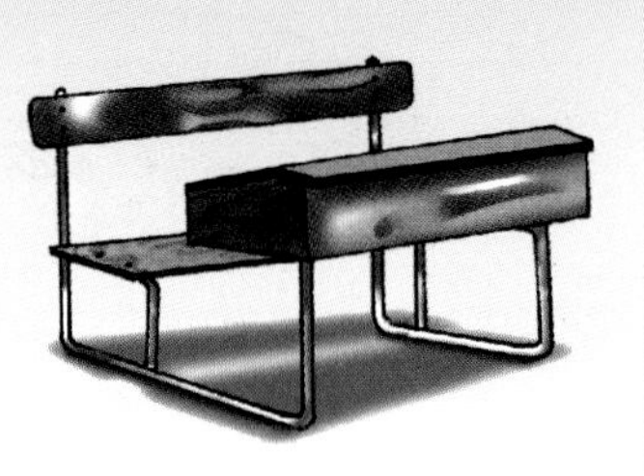

desk

مێز

miz

dish

ده وری

dawry

drawer

کومود

komod

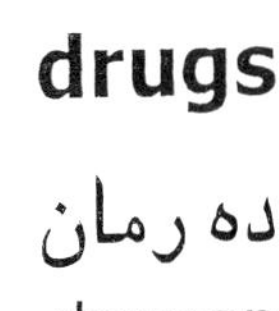

drugs

ده رمان

darman

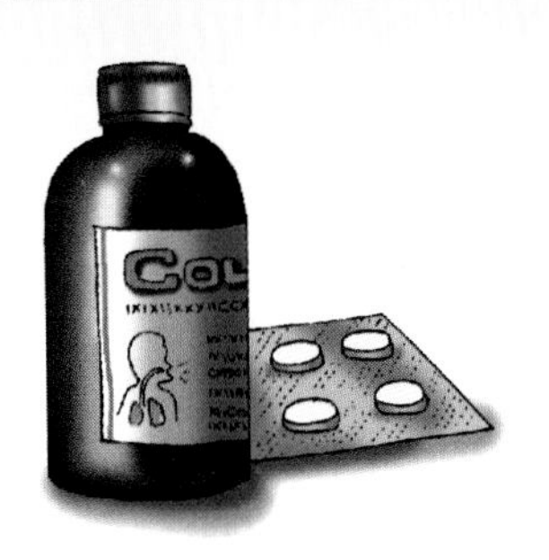

dustbin

سه تلی زبێل

satli zibil

envelopes

پاکه ت

pakat

eraser

پاك کون

pak kon

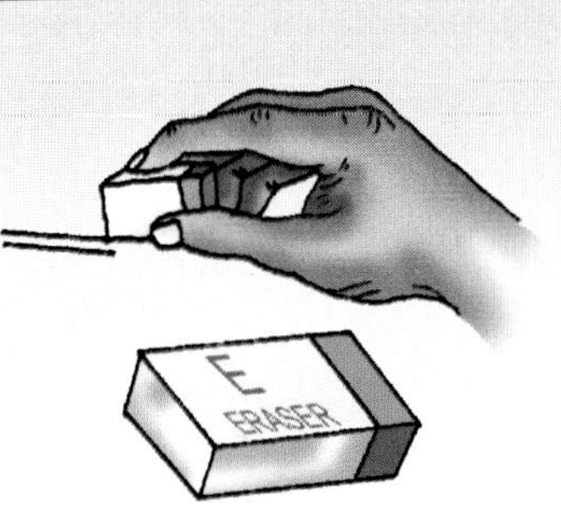

fans

باوه شێن

bavashin

fire
ئاگر
ager

flag
ئاڵا
alaa

fountain
فه واره
fawwara

fur (coat)
کۆت
kout

garbage
زبیل
zibil

gift

دیاری
diary

glass
لیوان–شوشه
liwan-shosha

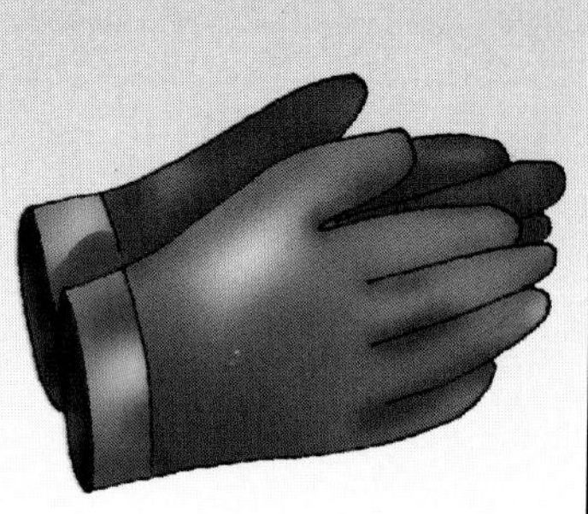

gloves
ده سته وانه
dastawana

goblet
جامی شراب
jamysharab

goggles

چاویلکه
chawelka

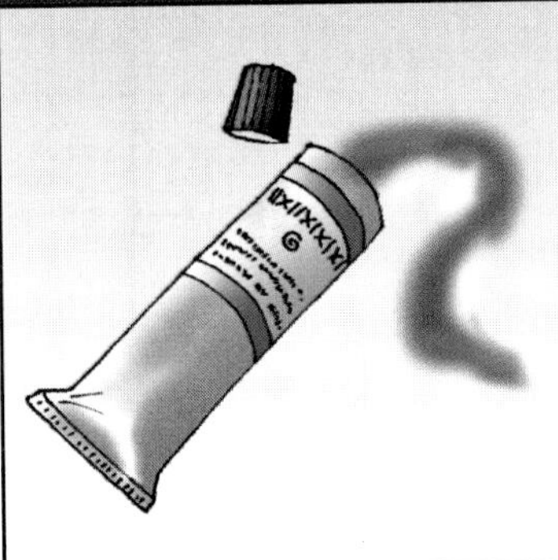

gum/glue

چه سب—چرێش

chasb-cherrish

guns

ده مانچه

damancha

hammer

چه کوچ

chakocha

handkerchief

ده سماڵ کاغه زی

dasmale kaghazy

handles

ده ستگیره

dastgira

hats

کڵاو

kolaw

helmet

کڵاوی ئاسن

kolawy asen

ink

مورره که ب

morrakab

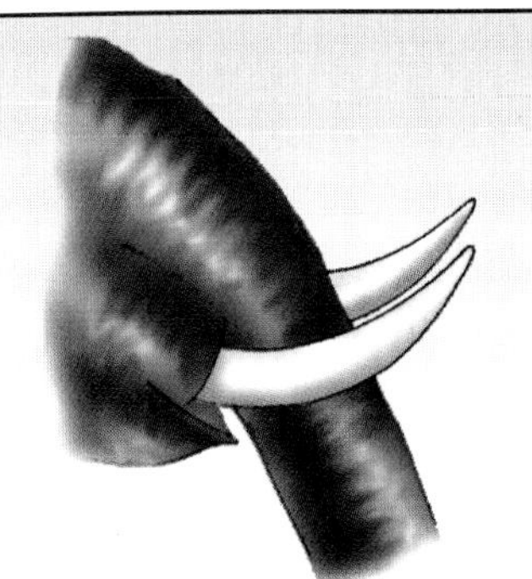

ivory

ئاجی فیل

ajy fil

jar

گۆزه

goza

jug
گوزه ڵه ی ئاوی
gozalay avi

kettle
که تری
katry

keys
هاچه ر
hachar

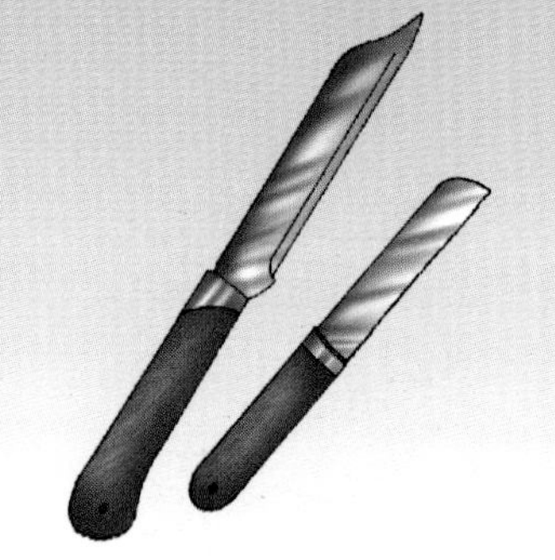

knives
چه قۆ
chaghow

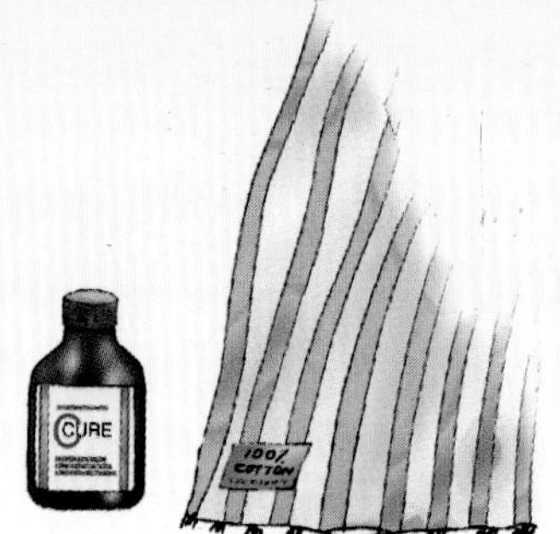

labels
نێشانه
nishana

lace

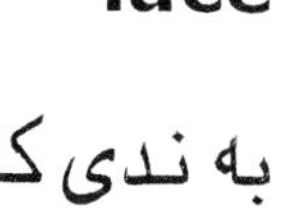

به ندی که وش
bandy kawsh

ladder
نه ردیوان
nardiwan

leather
چه رم
charm

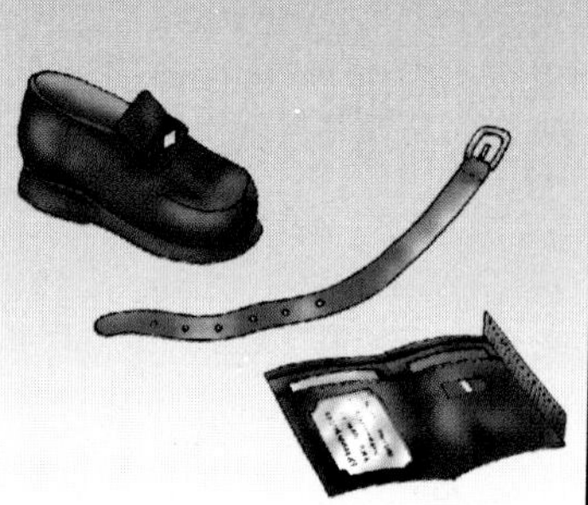

lens
زه ڕڕه بێن
zarrabin

letters

نامه
nama

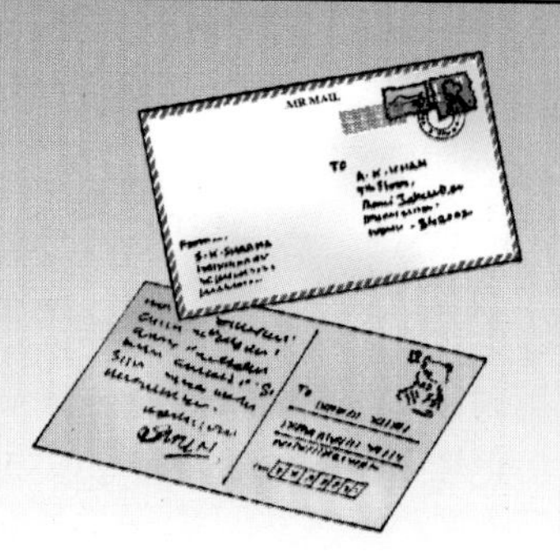

locks
قفل
ghefl

luggage
بارگه
bargha

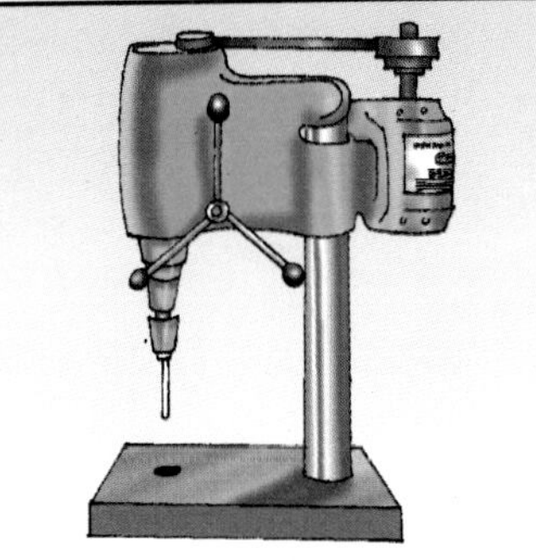

machine
ماشین
mashin

masks
رۆوبه ند
rowband

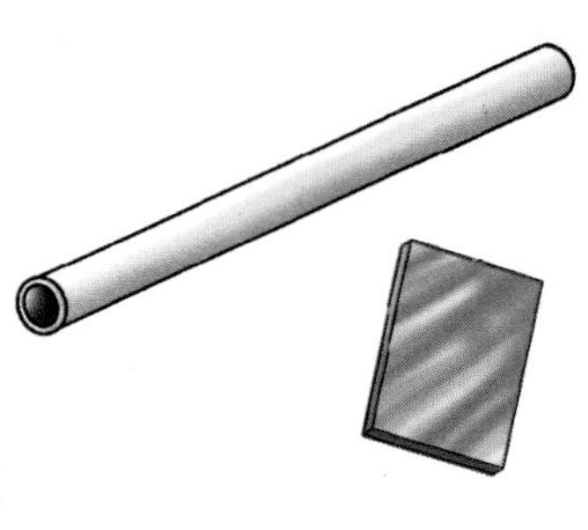

metal
فلز
felez

mirror
ئاوێنه
awena

money
پاره
para

mud
قور
ghor

mug
لیوانی گه وره
liwany gowra

napkin
ده سماڵی سفره ی
dasmaly sofrey

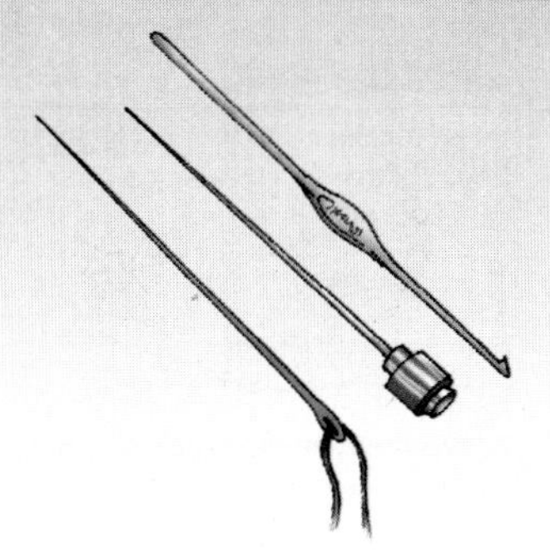

needles

ده رزی

darzy

nest

هێلانه

hellana

net

توور

toor

newspaper

رۆژنامه

rowjnama

oil

رۆن

rouwn

paint

ڕه نگ

rang

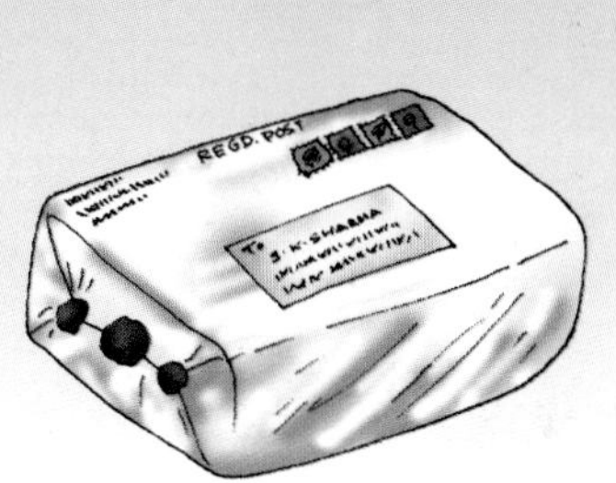

parcel

به سته ی پۆستی

basey posty

pedals

پێداڵ

pedal

pens

خودکار

khoudkar

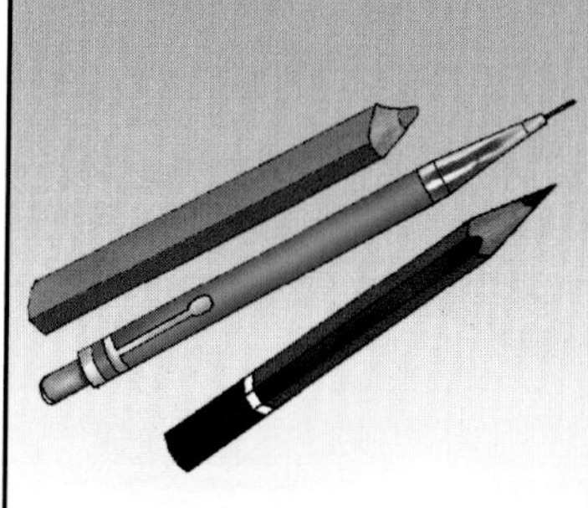

pencils

پێ نووس

peinous

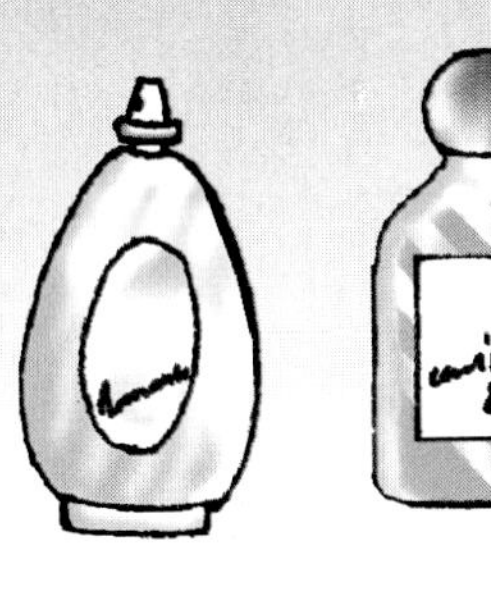

perfume

عه تر

atr

photograph

وێنه

wena

painting

وێنه کردن

wean kerden

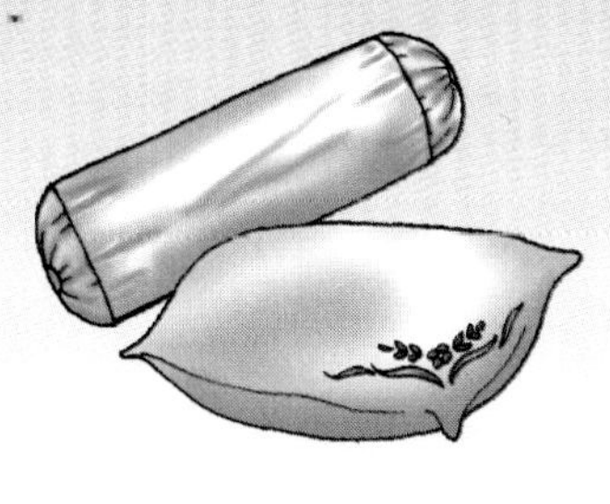

pillows

باڵنج

balenj

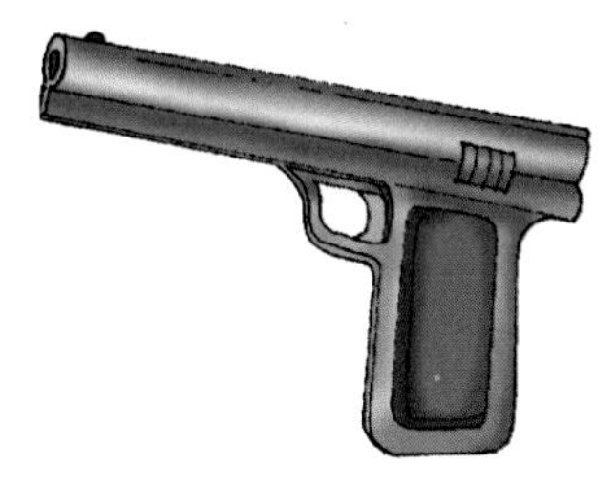

pistol

ده مانچه

damancha

plate

ده وری

dawry

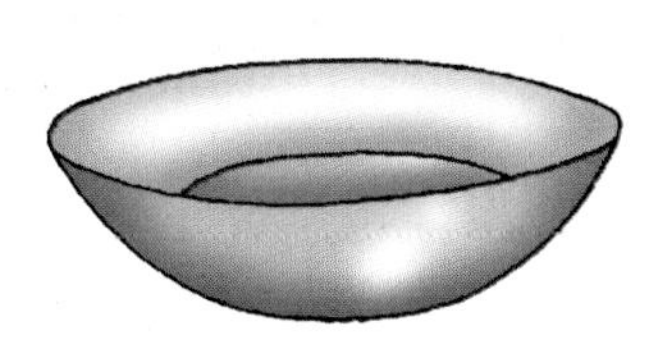

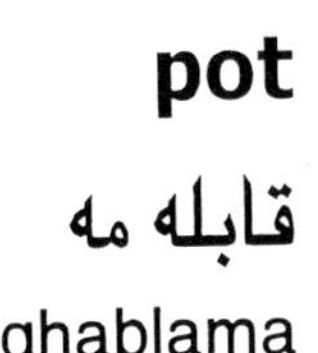

pot

قابله مه

ghablama

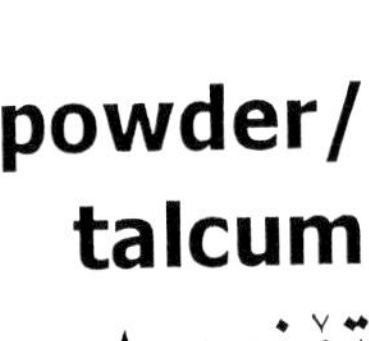

powder/ talcum

تۆز/پودر

touz-podr

pumps

پومپ

pomp

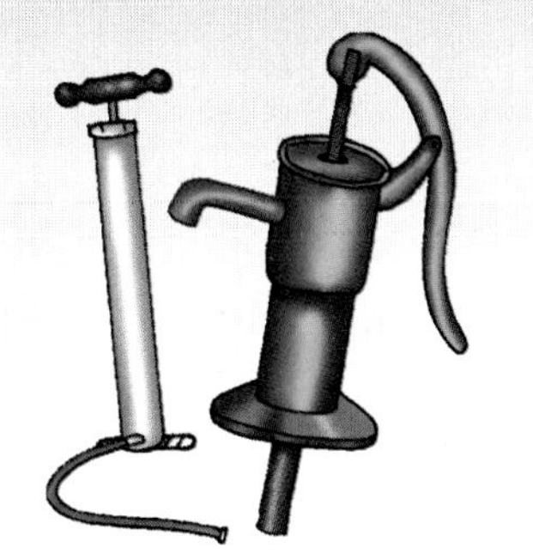

purse

کیفی پوولی ژنانه

kify poly jhenana

quilt
لێفه
lefa

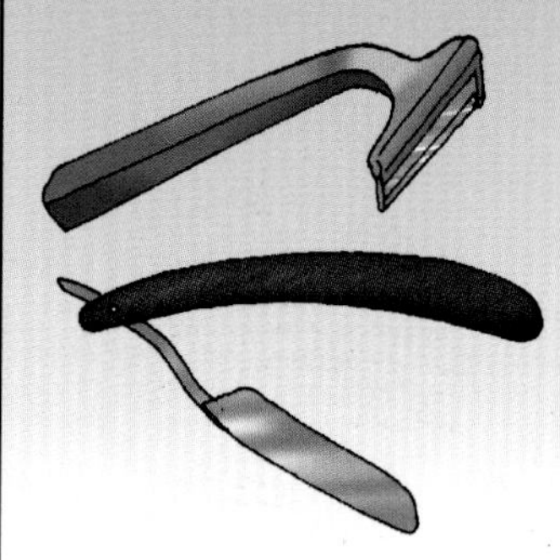

razors
تیغی تاشین
tighy tashin

refrigerator
یه خچاڵ
yakhchal

register
نانوسی
nawnusy

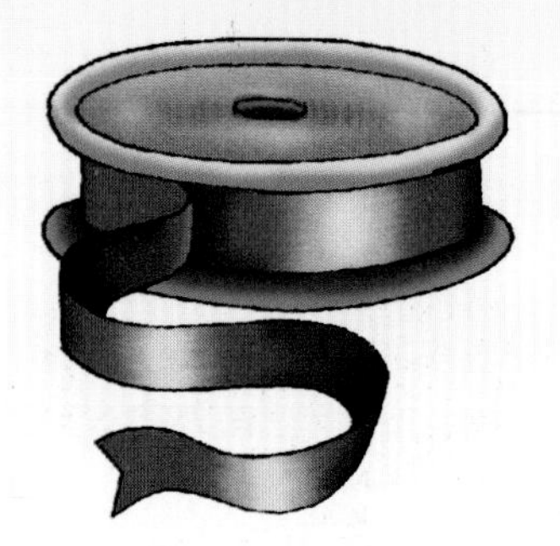

ribbon
ڕوبان
roban

robot
مرۆڤی ئاسن
merowfi asen

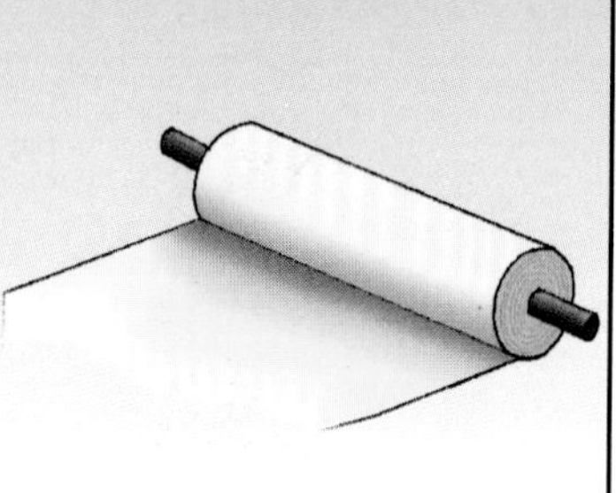

roll
تۆپ
towp

rope
ته ناف
tanaf

sacks
تۆربه
torba

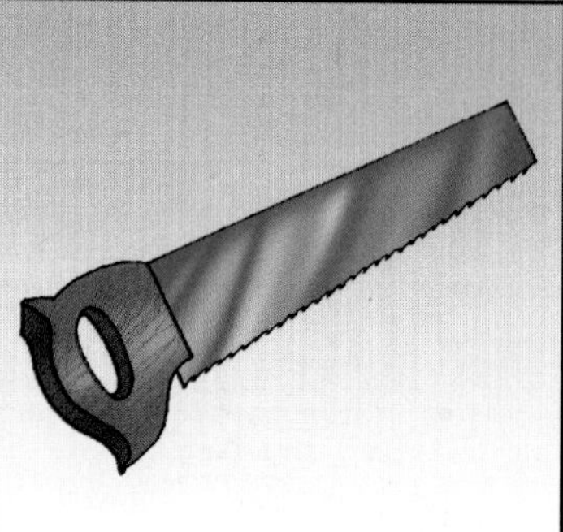

saw
مشار
meshar

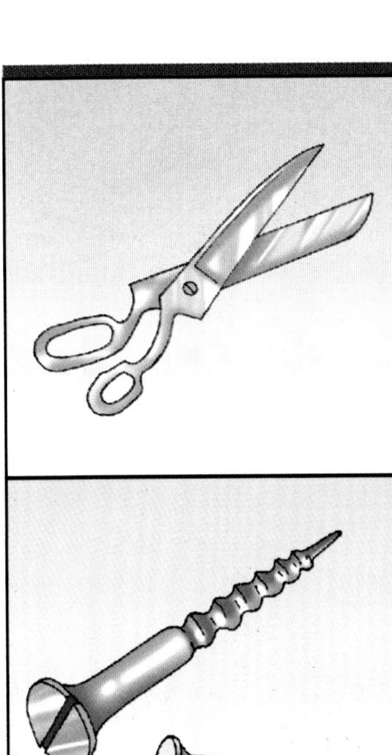

scissors

مه قه ست

maghast

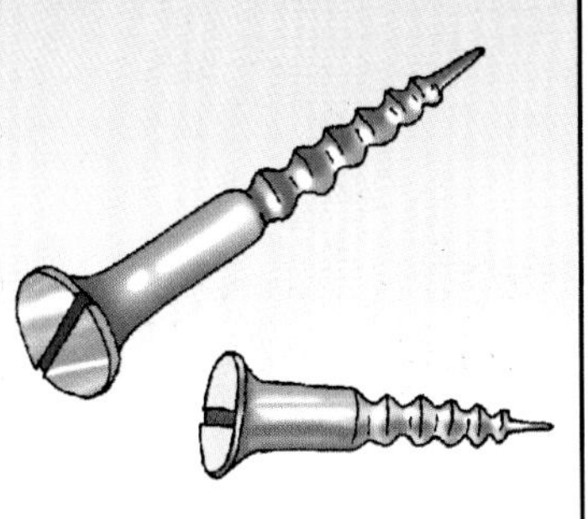

screws

پیچ

peich

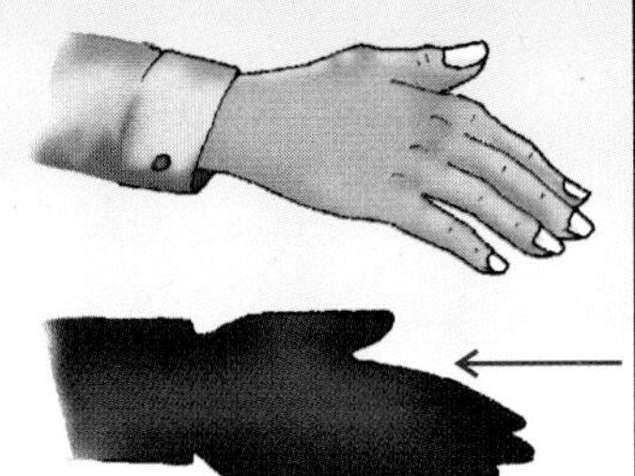

shadow

نیسێ

nisey

shampoo

شامپوو

shampoo

shirt

کراس

keras

shoes

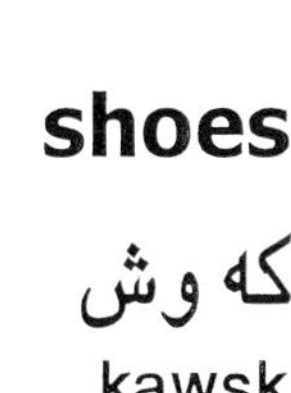

که وش

kawsk

slate

له وحی به ردی

lawhy bardi

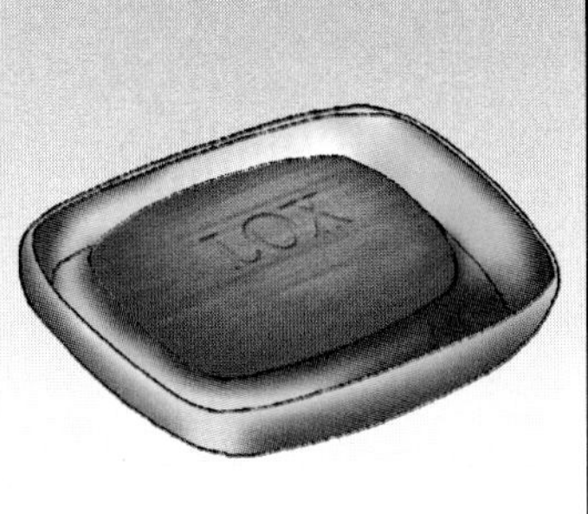

soap

سابوون

saboun

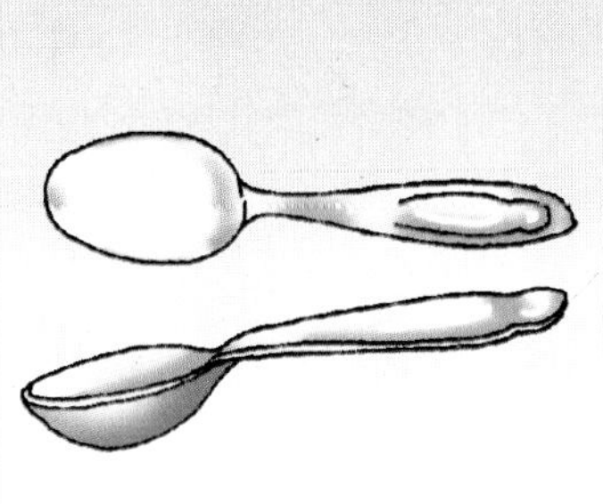

spoons

که وچك

kawchek

spray

پرژه

perjha

statue
په يكه ره
pay kara

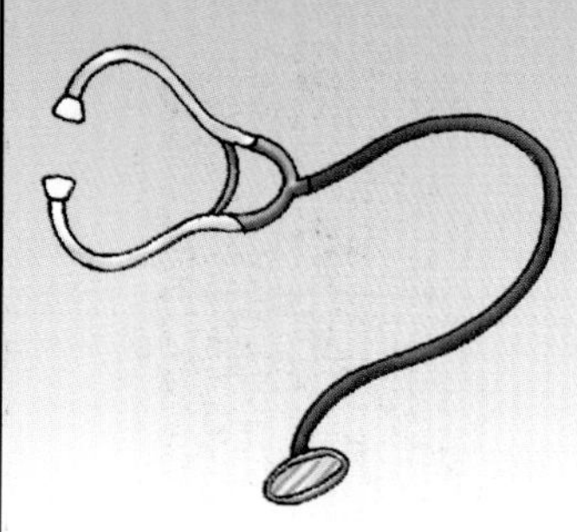

stethoscope
گۆشی دۆکتور
gowshi doktor

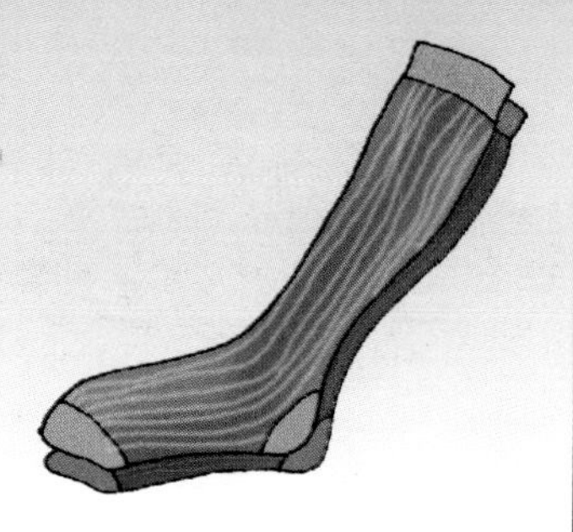

socks
گۆره وی
gorawy

teapot
چادان
chadan

thread
ده زوو
dazoo

tickets
بلێت
belit

timber
ئه لواد
alwar

tins
حه له بی
halabi

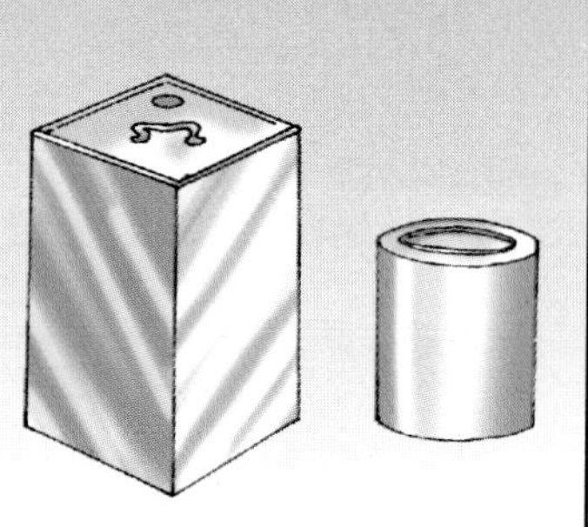

tools
ئالـات
alat

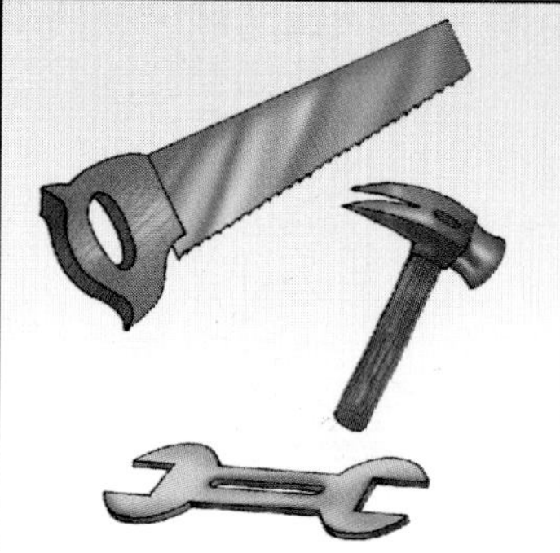

towels
خه ولی
khawly

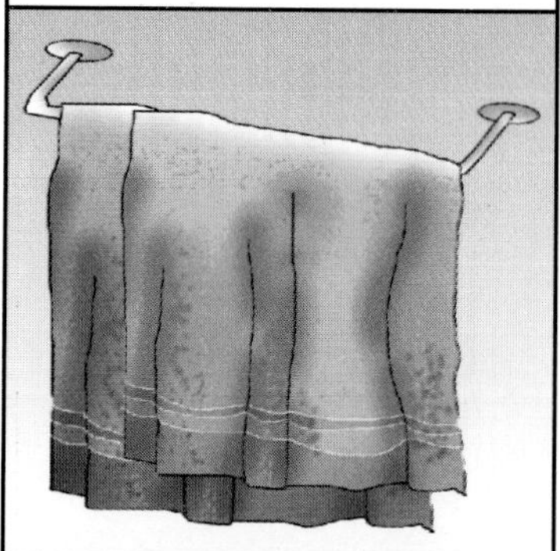

mousetrap

ته ڵه ی مشکی

taley meshky

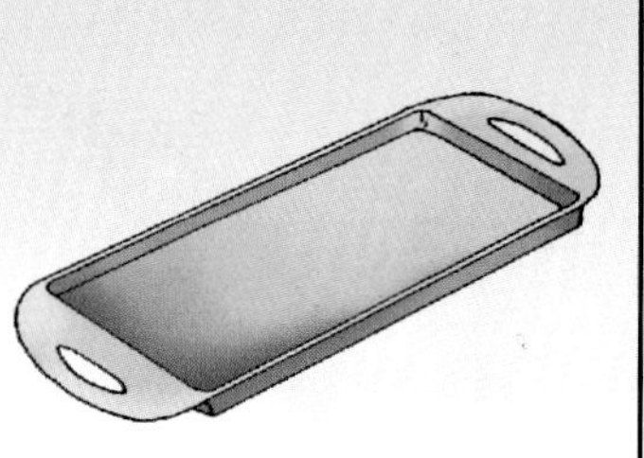

tray

سینی

siny

treasure

خه زێنه

khazina

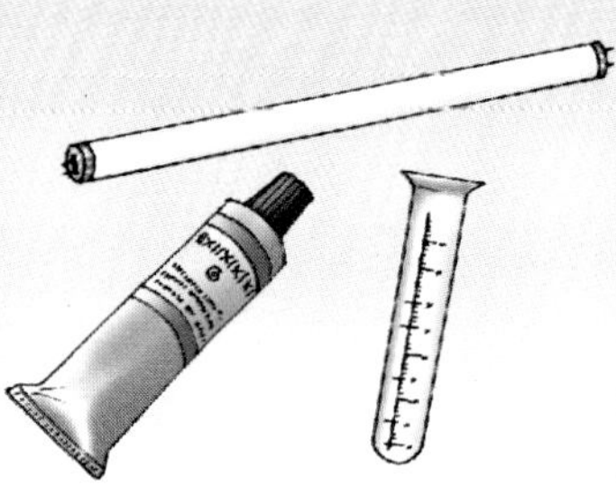

tubes

لوله

loula

turban

سه رپێچ

sarpech

typewriter

ماشێنی نووسێن

mashiny nousin

umbrella

چه تر

chart

utensils

قاب و که و چك

ghab o kawchek

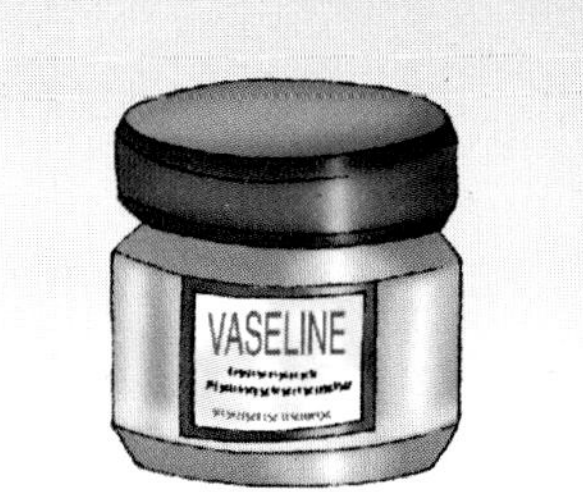

vaseline

وازلین

wazelin

vault

گومبه ز

gombaz

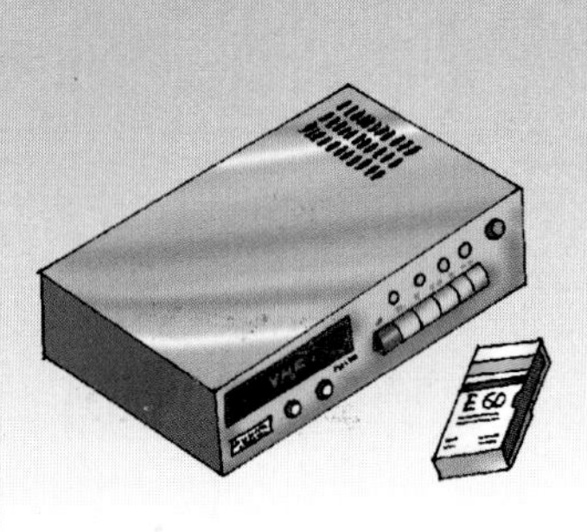

video machine
ویدئو
wideo

wallet
کیفی پووڵی
مرۆفان
kify pouli
merofan

washing machine
ماشینی جل شۆر
mashini jel
shour

watch
کات ئژ مێری مه
چه ك
katajhmiry
machak

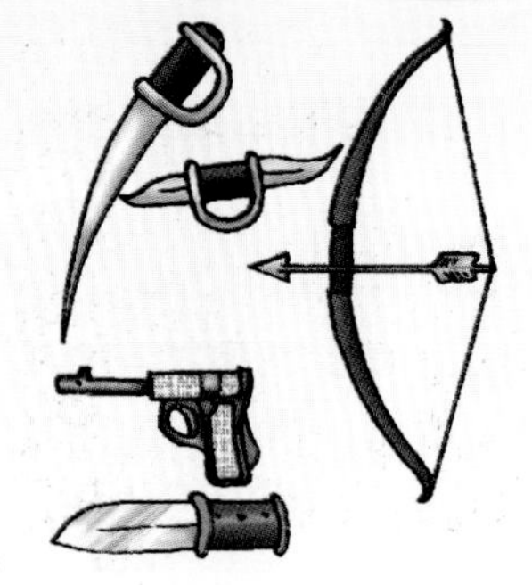

weapons
ئه سله حه
aslaha

web

تۆر
tour

wings
باڵی مه ل
baly mal

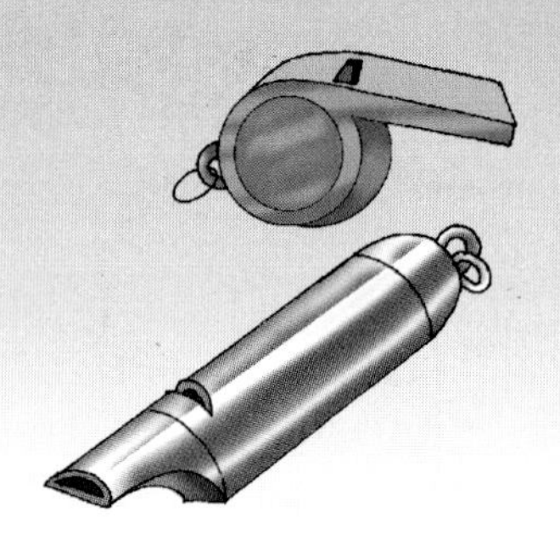

whistles
فیت فیته
fitfita

wool
په شم
pashm

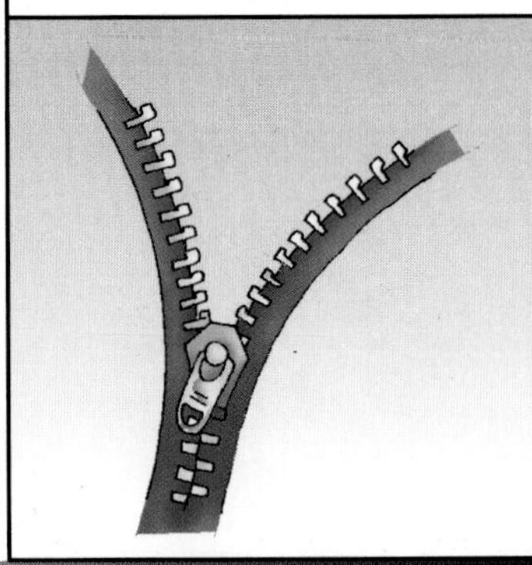

zipper
زیپ
zip